A Stranger In My Bed

By Kevin Luttery

BRYANT & DILLON PUBLISHERS
ORANGE, NEW JERSEY

As this is my first book, extending thanks is not an easy task, for my appreciation does not simply rest with those individuals who have directly contributed to this project, but I am indebted to so many who assisted, if only by moral encouragement, throughout the years leading to my writing this book. I would foremost like to thank my family for believing in me when I maintained that I was a writer. I would like to thank Kelsey Collie, Professor Lurns, Theodore Hudson and the many other faculty members at HU who enlightened and nurtured me during my four-year stay at the Mecca. Thank you Audrey Edwards and Diane Weathers at *Essence* magazine. Val—thanks for helping me exercise patience. Seyoum—your wisdom has not gone unheeded. Linda—thanks for not saying "I told you so." Thank you Gloria Wade-Gayles, Marie Brown and Emile Dillon Jr. for your educating me in this maddening business of book publishing. And of course, Vivian, Carole and Jocelyn—I thank you ladies for being such dear friends and attentive listeners.

A Stranger in My Bed
Copyright© 1997 by Kevin Luttery

Library of Congress Cataloging-in-Publication Data
Luttery, Kevin
1. Relationships 2.Ethnic/Minority 3.Non-Fiction
(A Bryant and Dillon Book)

CIP#97-75168
ISBN 1-889408-03-4

Edited by Tonya Martin
Interior Design by Laurie Williams/A Street Called Straight
Cover Design By Emile Dillon Jr./Digital Design

Publishers Note:
While this is a work of non-fiction, some of the name and locations have been changes to protect the identities of persons involved. Bryant and Dillon Publishers, Inc. shall have no liability to any persons or entities with respect to any information contained in this book.

Printed in the United States of America.
10 9 8 7 6 5 4 3 2 1

For Carmen.
Whose compassion and insight defy her youth
—KL

A Stranger in My Bed

Chapter One

Her name was Chris but it may as well had been Goldilocks. For like the Three Bears, I too found a stranger in my bed. I don't know how it happened. I don't know when it happened. All I know is that an attractive woman was pressed firmly against me and yet never before had I felt so cold and so alone. Yet this wasn't the amnesic result that often follows an empty one-night affair. In fact, the woman lying next to me was the same woman I had awakened to many mornings before. It was the same woman I referred to as my "lady friend." It was the same woman I even thought could perhaps one day be my wife and the mother of my child. But such visions escaped me as I lay staring at a woman I no longer knew. For the first time in our relationship, I could not see Chris simply as someone I had grown to love. I could not see the warmth and tenderness she tried to bring into my life. I couldn't even see the quiet beauty that so possessed me in the beginning. All I saw was that there was a White woman sleeping in my bed. Had someone told me that I would one day entertain the idea of spending the rest of my life with anyone other than a Black woman, I wouldn't have given it more than a passing thought. For, like so many of us, Black and White, I wanted to believe the myth that love conquers all, that despite external differences the only thing that truly matters is how two people feel about each other. And for a long time I subscribed to this very thought.

I told myself that a person's color was just that–it was color. And just as I never want to be judged by my color, nor was I going to be a judge. But such an attitude is at best overly optimistic and, worse, dangerously foolish. For such an attitude is the governing doctrine of an idealistic utopia, a state where color is meaningless and love is love. But I'm not an idealist living in utopia. I'm a Black man living in America, the result of which does not afford me the luxury of ignoring one's color and pretending that race no longer matters in this country.

As such, I found it increasingly difficult, and eventually impossible, to look beyond Chris's skin and simply see her for the person she claimed to be. It wasn't enough that I held true feelings for her. Nor was it enough that she often said she would do anything for the man she loved. For in the end, the only thing that mattered was whether or not I remained true to my beliefs, my feelings, my convictions. Whether or not I remained true to myself.

Yet during the nine months that Chris was in my life, truth eluded me. Somehow—in between the many hugs and kisses, breakfasts and dinners, late night rendezvous at her place or my place—I had lost a part of myself. Slowly and almost indiscernibly, what I initially mistook as self-gratification, personal growth, and fulfillment would later become a state of psychological erosion and decay. It would later become my very own metamorphosis.

I suppose I should have recognized the change overcoming me fairly early in the relationship. But I didn't want to recognize it. I thought that an admission of my feelings was an admission of my own racial beliefs and prejudices. I thus chose to ignore my feelings. Still, regardless of how cunning I was at suppressing the truth, not a day passed that I wasn't reminded, directly or otherwise, that my relationship with Chris had become sacrificial. It was as if I had to deny so much of who I was in order to avoid confrontation and thus make the relationship work. Although this was fine in the beginning, because I really did want to give us a fair chance, there would eventually come a day when I could no longer pretend not to feel so much of what I felt and still invite Chris into my bed.

The arrival of such a day is what I now regard as my personal epiphany. It was actually through talking with an ex-girlfriend that I was forced to admit to myself that something in my life was not right, that somehow or another I was no longer the man I had always been.

Jackie knew I had been seeing Chris since she and I split. In fact, it was our discussion about Chris that led to the disturbing event that would follow. Having long suspected Chris and I of sleeping together while she and I were dating, Jackie made no attempt to hide her feelings about my "White girlfriend." She called her names—dirty, foul names—and suggested things about her character that I did not want to believe. And of course I defended Chris, took her side and held Jackie at bay by laying claim that Chris was a better woman than she could ever be. Not to my surprise, this only heightened Jackie's discontent about the new woman in my life. Usually very soft-spoken and reserved, Jackie found the most indignant tone within her and asked, "Why are you even sticking up for that White woman?" I didn't bother to answer the question because it seemed almost rhetorical. I was sticking up for her because that is what people do who care for each other. And I did care about Chris. I cared deeply for her.

I also still cared for Jackie. Yet realizing that she and I had lost what little civility remained between us, I was hoping to end the conversation before it got any uglier. But Jackie wasn't interested in ending the conversation. She was too determined to have her say about the woman she claimed had come between us.

That's when it happened. As if spoken by an unseen ventriloquist, the words leaped from my mouth and hung heavy in the air. I tried to make amends with the catch-all "I'm sorry," but I knew nothing else I said could ever erase the pain I unwillingly inflicted on Jackie. I also knew that what was to follow would be my inevitable descent into a pit of psychological and emotional turmoil. I knew this the day I called the woman I had once tried to love a Black bitch.

Chapter Two

I would like to sound romantic and say
that it was fate that brought us together,
that Chris and I fell madly in love and simply could not
live apart. But I can't say any of that. Nor can I say that
I was just another confused brother running around
purposely looking for a White woman to give me what
I thought Black women were either unable or unwill-
ing to give. That too would be misleading. Yet my relationship with Chris was neither a deliberate choice nor
an accidental mishap. Things were never completely
black and white. Like the gray in Chris's eyes, the circumstance under which we got together was just as
obscure.

It all started in a writing workshop. Having spent
my first post–college year teaching high school English,
I decided to take a leave from the system and try to
establish myself as a serious writer. There was a very
good program offered at a nearby college that allowed

me the flexibility of attending classes while still working part-time as a substitute teacher

As it was the English department's goal to provide
very personal attention and instruction, the number of
students enrolled in the workshop was confined to
about fifteen. We were a pretty close-knit group, our
critique sessions often lingering beyond the allotted
classroom time, and ultimately spilling over into a nearby restaurant or bar.

The workshop was not only small, but also dis-
proportionately balanced gender wise. Because of this,
I found myself in academic and social settings where
the male–female ratio was easily one to four. Although
several of the women were quite attractive, none of
them really stood apart from the others. None of them
made me want her for the mere sake of wanting. None
of them, that is, except for Jackie.

Before the turning of tides swept me up and
washed me into Chris's life, it was Jackie who first stirred
emotions in me that for so long had lain dormant and
untouched. She was one of the prettiest women I had
ever seen and carried herself with all of the style, poise,
and dignity I seek in a woman. There was a quiet calm
about her that, in contrast with my loud and reckless
lifestyle, afforded me a sense of inner peace by merely
watching her from across the room. She was very shy
and demure but would still make her presence known
whenever she stepped into a room. At least I felt it.

Moving her body with the rhythmic and pulsating
gait so endemic to Black women, Jackie emitted an air
that suggested she had somewhere to be and wasn't
about wasting time in getting there. I suppose that is

why she rarely joined me and the rest of the students when we went out for drinks or lunch or got together and did nothing in particular. Instead, she would sneak off to the stacks and lose herself in a thick book. It was upon seeing this for the first time that I knew she was the type of woman I needed next to me. In addition to apple-firm tits or a perfectly round ass, there is nothing I find more arousing than an intelligent woman. And Jackie was intelligent. She was also very sexy.

Whenever the opportunity would present itself, I thus found some excuse to interrupt her whenever our paths crossed at the library. But the scene never unfolded the way I had rehearsed it in my mind. As I said, she was painfully shy and wasn't much of a talker. Given the choice, I believe she would have preferred that I had simply left her alone.

Sensing that I was more of a nuisance than a welcomed break from her studies, I would remove myself from the awkward silence and make that seemingly endless walk across the room back to my seat. I felt that every woman in the library was staring at me and that they all, like a Greek chorus in unison, echoed the same lamentation: "Kev gets no play today."

As embarrassed as I often was and as sophomoric as I must have appeared to Jackie, I had not resigned to throwing up my hands and walking away from it all. I wanted this woman and had already made up my mind that I was going to have her. Yet unlike my approach to some women in the past, I wasn't going to insult her with a bunch of lines that we both knew were no more original than they were sincere. And one thing I wanted to be with Jackie was sincere.

Having recently finished reading *Wild Women Don't Wear No Blues*, I thought that I would suggest the book to her and that maybe we could get together and discuss it. She was tucked away in her favorite corner when I approached her. Her legs were extended and propped on a chair, crossed at the ankles. She held her head slightly to one side, one hand stuffed between her knees, the other holding a book in front of her face.

"Hello," I said.

Jackie gave me a curious look and smiled. She removed her thumb from the center of the book and placed it face down on her naked thigh. Interested in the type of material she read, my eyes quickly fell onto the title. But it was her legs that held my true attention. I noticed how toned they were without appearing hard and manly. Her skin was an even, smooth, cocoa brown. I tried not to stare but stared nonetheless. Perhaps a little uncomfortable with the scrutiny of her body, Jackie shifted in her seat, uncrossed her ankles and then crossed them again.

"So how are you?" she asked.

I forced myself to make eye contact and said that I was doing fine. I then realized that I had been standing over her, book in hand, and lusty thoughts in my head that seemingly had no real purpose for being there. Running the risk of appearing too intrusive, I asked if it was okay if I sat down. She didn't bother to answer, but merely removed her feet from the chair and closed the book, her finger marking the page. She was reading Hugo's *Les Miserables* and was nearly finished.

"How is it?" I asked, nodding slightly toward the very fat paperback.

Again she didn't bother to answer but instead asked if I had read it. Having been an English teacher and a supposed writer, I was tempted to lie and say, "Yes, of course I've read it," followed by some pretentious comment on expressionism or realism or romanticism or some other literary concept every English teacher and writer should be able to discuss. But I wanted to be unaffected with Jackie. No lies. No games. No pretense. So I admitted that, "No, I haven't read it."

"You should read it," she said.

It was then that I applied my first litmus test. By loaning her the book I was holding—a collection of essays written by various Black women—I had not only hoped to spend time talking with her about the work, but it was also my intention to gain an insight as to the type of woman she was, as well as to discover those beliefs and convictions she held closest to her heart.

Jackie took the book, flipped through it for a moment, and thanked me for sharing it with her. She said that it looked interesting enough and that she would definitely read it. But I wasn't expecting very much. Having loaned women books in the past, I knew that this gesture was quite often met with the polite return of the book several weeks later, and a generic apology about "not being able to get into it" or something like that.

But Jackie was different. Two days after I loaned her the book she returned it to me, having read it cover to cover. I recall spending all of three weeks reading the same book. Although not a death-defying feat, her taking the time to read the book, and having read it so quickly, was extremely attractive to me. In fact, I was so attracted to her at that moment that my emotions were able to allay any trepidation I may have had about asking if she wanted to get together some time. The night she returned my book was the same night I got her phone number. Not worrying if I appeared too eager or too desperate or too anything, I called her the very next day.

Much as I suspected, conversation with Jackie was initially very lopsided. Holding very old-fashioned, or in her words "traditional" values, Jackie felt that men should be the initiators and that it was their responsibility to "make the first move." Such a philosophy was evident in the way she later approached our relationship.

If I wanted to talk to her, then I was the one who usually picked up the phone and called. And, once I did, it was I who carried the responsibility of starting the conversation and keeping it going. Because she was so shy, there were times when I felt like I was on stage delivering a Shakespearean soliloquy, my endless talk sporadically broken with an occasional "uh-huh," "I see," or some other interjection indicating that she was still listening. And though she didn't speak very often, when she did it was because she had something of real significance to say.

Conversation notwithstanding, my relationship with Jackie had what I considered to be a very firm base on which to later build. Though some might say things were actually slow and undramatic, it was, if anything, my intention to have them as such. Prior to meeting Jackie, I had been involved with several women who were nothing more than a sexual conve-

nience or someone to help fill the empty space. But I
didn't want Jackie in my life like that. I had recently
turned twenty-three, and I felt I had gotten most of that
youthful wildness out of my system, and that it was
time I had something real and stable.

Though I was not in a rush to run out and get married the next day, I knew that I wanted to be settled by
the time I turned thirty, and that I wanted to settle with
one of the many fine sisters running around Atlanta.
Jackie wanted this as well. The only problem was that
there were a few things she had to work out within
herself before she could even think about getting married and starting a family.

Five years my senior, Jackie admitted that she had
a difficult time trusting me. She thought that because I
was so much younger than she, that surely the only
thing I was interested in doing was getting between her
legs. After all, so her reasoning went, that's the attraction most young guys have for older women.

Understanding that her fear was both real and
valid, I tried to show—not lip the words but actually
show—that I was genuinely interested in who she was
as a person. I thought that she was pretty. She was
smart, well-read, classy, and sexy. She was a lady. And
I wanted this lady. I wanted her next to me, holding my
hand, laughing, playing, enjoying life. For these
reasons, I was not only willing to forgo sex, but I knew
that I had to forgo it. Jumping in bed with Jackie before
taking time to understand who she was and what she
was about would only distort things. Sex too soon ran
the risk of creating a false sense of emotion. And I was-
n't willing to risk this. I needed to be certain that I was

truly interested in Jackie and not just in Jackie's coochie.

By waiving sex, I thus had ample occasions to get to know her during those initial few weeks. We went to the park, to the movies, had breakfast, lunch and dinner. We had gone out for nearly a month before we ever shared our first kiss. As unbelievable as this sometimes seems to me now, I admit that I was quite happy without the physical involvement, that simply being in her company was enough. It was what I wanted; it was what we both wanted. And it was necessary if I were to gain her trust.

Later, once I had convinced her that she could trust me and that my sole objective wasn't to screw her, she began to relax and extend a little more of herself. She even began to talk. For the most part Jackie and I held what people often call "deep" conversations. We talked about books we'd read, courses we had taken in college, social and political events in the news. We talked about things we had written and things we had planned to write. One thing we rarely talked about was Jackie herself.

Whenever I made an effort to get her to open up to me—not spill her guts and share every dark secret she carried inside, but to simply open up and show me a little more of who she was—her initial reaction was to get defensive and question my motive. But there was no motive. "I'm just trying to get to know you," I repeated to her. Sure, we were both working hard toward that end, and we certainly had made progress. But it was evident that she was not yet ready to shut the door on her past and give her complete trust to me.

At twenty-eight, Jackie was naturally carrying her share of collected baggage. If Freud's theory was correct in that one's childhood is the premise upon which one later constructs his/her adulthood, then surely such psychology played a fundamental role in Jackie's life.

We were lying on my bed one day when Jackie opened up to me for the first time and admitted that she not only had a hard time trusting me, but that she didn't trust men in general. She was lying on top of me with her face lightly pressed into the crease of my neck. I could feel her slow, steady breath against my ear, matched by the rise and fall of her body against my body. As she spoke in false starts and hesitations, I could feel the hot tears as they ran down her face and slowly dripped against my bare skin. I dared not speak and lay perfectly still holding her as close as I could. As if her deep moans served as a mystical incantation, Jackie reached into her soul and conjured up those demons that had haunted her for so many years.

She went on to tell me that when she was younger her father had beaten her mother and that it was, quite disturbingly, a common practice of most of the men in her family to beat on their women. As she spoke that first revelation, I fought to suppress that "uh-oh" feeling that often accompanies the early recognition of bad things to follow. But I couldn't suppress it, for I knew that the past of which Jackie spoke would loom over our future like a dark cloud, an ominous foreshadowing of potential problems we would later face in the relationship.

Although I knew there were men who beat the women they claim to love, I was not such a man. I had never known such a man. There was, therefore, nothing I could say to Jackie that would express an understanding of what she was feeling. But I tried to understand. I lay there holding her, and I tried to understand how the events of her past had made her the woman she was today.

Before it was all over, Jackie told me that her father had not only beaten her mother, but that when Jackie was no more that ten he had walked out on them. The distrust that this event caused was further reinforced by the few, albeit quite traumatic, relationships she had had with men as a young adult.

Forever under the overprotective eye of her mother, she never had much experience dating while growing up. She even claimed to had only been sexually involved with three men her entire life. At first I found such a statement incredulous, but I would later accept it as the truth. As painful as it must have been for her, Jackie admitted that she had once been engaged, only to have her fiancé call her to announce that he had just married another woman. Neither she nor her mother had ever forgiven him, which was all too obvious in Jackie's current perception of men. Such a perception was even more distorted by her brother's irresponsible behavior.

As a young man Jackie's brother had fathered a child, refused to marry the woman, and then found excuse not to support his little girl. He would later father another child by a different woman and, due to the pressure of his mother, grandmother, sister, and probably every other woman in the family, joined the grossly misunderstood institution of marriage. As noble as this may appear outwardly, the marriage wasn't without its problems. Seemingly an imitation of his father, Jackie's brother drank too much and worked too little. The time in between was spent kicking his wife's ass.

Living in the same house as her brother, his wife and their daughter, as well as her mother and grandmother, Jackie expressed her frustration about always having to intervene when the fighting broke out and try to pull apart the exact two people she and her family had pushed together. Constantly reminded the way "all men are" by her overbearing mother, and by the reality of her abusive brother, Jackie said that she would walk away from a man rather than subject herself to such treatment.

Jackie didn't have to say another word. She had already made it perfectly clear that she was no silly little girl who would allow me to treat her however my mood dictated on any given day. I was well aware that from that point on Jackie could not help but look at me and see her ex-fiancé, her doggish brother, and so many other Black men from whom little more is expected than the worst.

Still, I wasn't going to write this relationship off as a no-win situation. I was going to remain optimistic that her one-dimensional perception of me was something we both could work through. The only problem, as I would later find out, is that the perceived sometimes holds more truth than the actual. Anticipation is like footfalls down an empty corridor, loud reverberations of where we've been and where we're headed. Anticipation grows out of the mind.

Chapter Three

Autumn fell upon us and brought with it all of its unmatched beauty. It's always been my favorite time of year, a time that, unlike any other season, deeply moves me with its vibrant colors and pungent aromas. Yellow, red, and orange leaves slowly drifted from above and sprinkled the ground like little fragments of a dream. That's how I felt as I stood in the midst of it all and simply held Jackie's hand. I felt like we were suspended in a dream.

It was a very cool October morning. Having just gotten out of class, Jackie and I lingered in the parking lot for a while. We talked and laughed and then we talked some more. I suggested she come back to my place and we continue the conversation there. Mornings like that were never meant to be experienced alone. They had to be shared for the moment and cherished thereafter. That's what I had in mind when I invited Jackie back to my apartment. I wanted to share something with her.

Jackie had been suffering from writer's block. I wanted her to forget about the novel she had been working on and simply relax. I also wanted to help her do just that. I ran her a warm papaya bubble bath and served her a cup of steaming tea. While she soaked in the tub, I busied myself in the kitchen whipping up a batch of pancakes and frying a few strips of bacon. Between my opening and closing cabinet doors, banging pans around and performing the other necessities of fixing breakfast, I could hear the faint splash of water shifting back and forth in the tub. It was a familiar sound, a soothing sound, a sound I wanted to hear again and again.

Jackie was lying back with her head resting against the wall when I went into the bathroom several minutes later to check on her. With her tea nearly finished and her eyes closed, she looked like a small piece of serenity itself. It was the same calm that first held me fixated in class as I watched her from across the room. I stood there for a while and relished the moment.

"How do you feel?" I asked.

She slowly opened her eyes and tried adjusting them to the light. She had that puzzled, almost confused, look one wears when awakened from a dream.

"Mmmm," she moaned, "I was about to fall asleep."

"Come on there will be plenty of time for that later," I said, opening a thick towel and inviting her to step in.

Jackie hesitated for a moment and stared deeply into my eyes. I knew what she was thinking because I was thinking the same thing. Not only had I not slept with Jackie at that point in our relationship, but I hadn't even seen her undressed. We both knew and felt that her stepping out of the tub was a symbolic step away from her troubled past and a step toward the future she and I were trying to build together.

Apparently wanting it just as much as I, Jackie rose from beneath the protective shield of bubbles and stood before me. That distinct "guussshhh!" sound that comes when one stands in a tub reverberated in my head as I watched the water stream down her naked body. There were a few scattered patches of foamy soap still covering parts of her, but those places that remained exposed glistened from the papaya oil that had soaked into her skin. Had I been a frog, I would have shot my tongue out and licked her body dry. But my luck that day didn't include taking on the persona of an amphibian. So I simply extended the towel further in Jackie's direction as she willingly stepped forth.

I gently wrapped her in the towel as I would an innocent baby who has never known the harsh realities of this world, and slowly began drying her off. Once done, I led her into the bedroom where a copy of the morning paper lay waiting on a pillow. She stretched her thin body across the bed and began scanning the front page headlines. All I could do for several minutes was stand at the doorway and watch her. I couldn't help noticing how comfortable and at home Jackie appeared. There was a natural ease in her demeanor that suggested she was where she was supposed to be. It was as if she belonged in my company and in my life. I envisioned coming home after dealing with the many worries of the world and finding her just like that, calm yet assured, relaxed though not idle, a small piece of peace waiting in my bed.

"Read it aloud," I said.

Jackie began sharing with me one of several non-descript articles about a nondescript person who had committed a nondescript crime. As she did so, I gently massaged her feet in preparation for the pedicure I was about to give her. It was a very strange dichotomy—Jackie reading of a world fraught with violence and rage—yet there we lay in our own little world temporarily removed from it all. It felt good. Not only the quiet calm, but it felt good in itself to treat Jackie as she deserved to be treated.

She was a lady, a very fine lady, and I wanted to treat her as such. I wanted to pamper her, caress her, take care of her. I wanted to simply love her.

It was during such tender moments that my grandmother's presence would intrude upon my space. A very wise woman, my grandmother often cautioned me about treating Black women too kindly. She said that in a Black women's eyes, a nice, loving, attentive man was all too often construed as a weak man. She further maintained that once I lavish her with such attention, especially if no man has ever extended this to her before, a Black woman would not only expect this of me, but she would demand it. And she would demand more and more and more.

"You can't let them run over you, Kev," my grandma warned.

"You have to be firm and stand up to them. Put your foot down and say, 'This I will do, this I won't do.' Because if you treat a Black woman too nicely, she'll take you for a chump and try to do with you whatever she can."

As much as I love and respect my grandmother, and as much as I need a great deal of her sage advice, I try as best I can to ignore such sweeping generalization. And this was particularly so with Jackie. As far as I was concerned, Jackie was a beautiful, Black princess. She was my princess, and every princess should have nothing less than a man willing to pamper her needs and desires. I thus pushed grandma to the recesses of my mind and tried to give Jackie all of my attention.

"Take that off," I said.

Jackie tossed the paper onto the floor, stood and peeled the towel from around her body. She slowly crawled back onto the bed as I instructed her to lie on her stomach, her face deeply buried in a pillow. Once I finished her feet, I turned to the rest of her body.

Her skin was moist and supple from the warm bath she had just taken. I dribbled a thin stream of oil onto her back and continued the massage. Her body felt good between my hands. I rubbed at the tension lodged at the base of her neck, moved a little lower between her shoulder blades and then slowly worked my way down her back. As I alternated between gentle strokes and firm caresses, I thought about the last time Jackie was lying on my bed and how, in telling me about the demons of her past, she had filled the room with the sound of aching grief. This time the low moans that escaped from beneath the pillow were of a much different kind.

With her moans of desire serving as a guide, I slid my hands from her back onto the fullness of her butt, squeezing and kneading it like a mound of clay, my fingers digging deeply into her soft flesh and then briefly pausing to gently massage the inside of her thighs. As her moans grew louder, my caress grew stronger, and the closeness took us a step further into our world.

"Turn over," I said.

Jackie rolled over onto her back and caught my eye. I slowly shifted my gaze down, up and back down her body. Her breasts, though small, were round and firm. She had a very thin waist that led into full, curved, luscious hips. A Black woman's hips. She lay exposed and vulnerable. She lay waiting to take the next step into our little world. I crawled on top of Jackie and pressed my body into her body. With our eyes filled with passion and our hearts filled with emotion, she and I shared the love we had been carrying around inside of us for far too long. We got into each other, next to, on top of, and around each other.

The sex we shared that morning seemed ancient, almost timeless. It seemed to transcend the immediate and breathe life into a distant past. Each touch, stroke, and movement flowed between us as if we had known each other's body just as long and intimately as our very own. But there had been no rehearsal to this occasion. It was all natural. What Jackie and I shared were common loose ends, an unspoken desire bound together by circumstance.

We would later eat breakfast and I would finish the pedicure I had begun. But for a long time she and I did nothing but hold each other close. It was reminiscent of the last time I held Jackie in my arms. Yet this time there were no tears. Unfortunately, there would come a day when the tears would return, a day when our quiet calm would be broken by the thunderous storm gaining force around us. But for right now there was only peace and love in our world. For right now the demons lay at rest.

Chapter Four

There is a sixth sense some women possess that seems to make them just a little more perceptive, just a little more in tune than most men. For it never fails that whenever I'm involved with a woman, every other woman around me can somehow sense this. Upon doing so, these overly intuitive women seem to all of a sudden find me irresistibly attractive. I receive sensuous looks in the grocery store that I never receive when I'm unattached. I have women stop me on the street asking for directions to a building that's clearly within sight. I'm approached in parking lots, conveniently bumped into at the gym, caught in the unrelenting stare as I wait for the traffic light to turn green.

I don't know if it's that such a woman, keenly sensing that my heart and attention are elsewhere, perceives me as untouchable, and this in turn rekindles her childhood desire to want what she can't have. Or is it as simple as a woman's propensity to introduce disruption and chaos into another woman's life by getting involved with an already involved man. I don't know. But what I do know is that Chris was certainly one of these women who had acquired such an extra sense.

It was shortly after Jackie and I shared our first sexual encounter that I began noticing Chris. Actually, I noticed her noticing me. I was at The Loft, a trendy bar and grill near campus where several up-and-coming writers and I often met to have a few beers and talk a lot of shit. I was headed home one day when I decided to stop by for a Beck's and see if I might could put a few words down on paper. Digging through my satchel for a pen, I suddenly experienced that strange sensation of being watched. I glanced around to identify the voyeur and, sure enough, caught Chris standing behind the bar with her eyes fixed on me.

I had been coming to The Loft for several months, and realized that I had not seen this woman working there in the past. Not thinking very much of it, my natural reaction was to simply return a polite exchange of eye contact and then resume what I had started. *She must be new*, I thought to myself. And that was that.

Despite the obvious that Chris was quite attractive, it never occurred to me that I would ever be interested in getting involved with her. And this wasn't because she was White. It was simply that I was seeing Jackie, and she was my sole focus. Of course, like so many men, there had been a time in my life that I tried to juggle more than one woman at once. But not anymore. Ever since Jackie and I had gotten together, the days of casually running through women became something foreign to me. Having made up my mind to slow down and take relationships more seriously, I told myself that I would no longer form casual liaisons, insignificant relationships with women who were not marriage material. It made no sense, at this stage in my life, to invest time and emotion in a woman I would not want to introduce as my wife. And Jackie was definitely intended to be someone's wife. She was intended to be my wife.

It was a couple of days after we slept together that I asked her to help me pick out a gift for my little niece. It was Ashleigh's third birthday, and I wanted to get her something really cutsie and girlie, unlike the toys and Dr. Suess books I'd gotten her in the past. Although I knew the saleslady could help in putting together a nice outfit, I deliberately invited Jackie along to apply the litmus test. I wanted to see, first of all, if she would even be interested in going with me to pick out a gift. And if so, just what type of taste did she have when it came to dressing a little girl.

She had once told me that her maternal instinct was very strong. Such was an indirect way of proving it, I thought as we browsed through the many racks of blouses, skirts and dresses. And she was right. As if she had done it a thousand times before, Jackie mixed and matched various pieces until finally arranging three very pretty outfits. That same warm feeling overcame me that I'd felt only a few days earlier when she lay in my bed reading the paper. I imagined the two of us at the store shopping for our own little girl. She would hold a piece of clothing in the air for my opinion.

"Kevin, what do you think about this?" she'd say.

"It's cute," would be my response. "It's really cute."

I stood there engrossed in a very simple yet engaging moment. Once Jackie had given me a small glimpse of how life might be if we ever truly got together, she and I stepped to the cash register and back into the real world. The saleslady made some comment that inferred she thought Jackie and I were married. I quickly corrected her, stating that, "No, we're not married. This is my fiancée." The words felt good rolling off my tongue. And they sounded good. Jackie wasn't one who quickly showed emotion, but on that particular occasion she had no choice. Emotion was spread all over her face. I could see it in her eyes and I could feel it in her body. I pulled her close to my side as she and I walked from the store. I was oblivious to everything around us as we strolled through the mall pressed up against one another. I felt that we weren't simply together. It was more than that. *Yes*, I silently mused to my self, *this is what I've been looking for.*

With that open admission that Jackie was the woman I wanted by my side, I was thus able to dismiss Chris's stares as mere curiosity. Even if they were looks of attraction, my reasoning was, the attraction was not mutual. I knew what I wanted. I had what I wanted. Everything else remained in the background, like the slow buzz of a November fly that senses its impending death.

But such a way of looking at things was far too simple. For just as I had made up my mind that I had to get next to Jackie, so too did Chris hold the same resolve for me.

I was at The Loft one night working on an essay. The writing was going along free and easy the way it does when a piece takes on true identity and nearly writes itself. I was lost in my compulsive scribbling of words when Chris's own words intruded upon my space.

"I've been watching you," she said.

I lifted my eyes and caught her stare as she stood over my booth.

"Excuse me?" I said.

"I've been watching you. Not like that or anything. It's just that I see you in here a lot writing."

I didn't say anything. It was obvious she was waiting for a response but I didn't have one. After all, how does one respond to, "I've been watching you?"

"So," she continued, "are you like a writer or something?"

"I write a little."

"Oh yeah?"

"Um-hm."

I took a swallow from my beer as I waited for the next generic question.

"So what do you write?" she asked.

"Essays."

"Oh," she said, a touch of disappointment in her soft voice. I suppose admitting to writing essays didn't sound as impressive as being a novelist or playwright or whatever. There was a moment of awkward silence, and then: "You know," she confided, "I've always wanted to be a writer."

"Is that so?"

"Yeah, I almost majored in English in college. I decided to study speech pathology instead."

I raised my eyebrows in surprise.

"But, as you see," she continued, "I'm not actually doing anything with my degree."

"You wait tables full time?"

"Just for now. Until I figure out what I really want to do."

"There's nothing wrong with that."

"No, I guess not."

"How long have you been out?"

"I just finished this year. Thought I would take a little time off before either getting a real job or going back to school."

"You think you might be interested in grad school?"

"I don't know, it's a thought."

There was another moment of strained silence.

"Well," she said,"I better get back to work."

She turned to leave but then hesitated for a moment.

"By the way, I'm Chris."

She slowly extended her hand in my direction. I politely returned the gesture.

"I'm Kevin."

"It was nice talking to you. I'm sure I'll be seeing you around."

"Yeah, I'm sure."

Chris crossed the room and began taking drink orders from a couple who had just been seated in her section. Although that initial scene was brief and rather uneventful, it would still leave an impression on me. There was a mysterious air about Chris that stayed on my mind long after I left The Loft.

Her movements and gestures were very slow, delib-erate, and calculated. She exuded a presence about her that often reminded me of a cat. Her gray eyes were like a thin veil to so much that lay beneath the surface, suggesting without telling, a subtle invitation that drew one in for closer inspection.

While lounging around my apartment later that night, I would find my attention drifting back to The Loft and replaying the scene over in my head. I turned her words this way and that, trying as best I could to recapture any inflection in her voice that may have given meaning to an otherwise meaningless exchange. My conclusion was that that's all it was—a meaningless exchange. There was nothing calculated going on, no ulterior motive lurking low in the grass. I had to remind myself that it was innocent and harmless. But this never came easy for me. As a young Black man in America, it was my nature to question everything and everyone around me. Chris was no exception.

In fact, I actually found myself questioning her more than I would an average person. First of all, she was White, and secondly, she was a woman, both of which have always raised suspect in the back of my mind. But I didn't want to judge too broadly or too quickly. And I admit that I was curious about this woman who kept her eyes fixed on me.

A few classmates and I were at The Loft having one of our informal critique sessions. Chris had been serving us drinks all night long but she and I never had a chance to really talk. It was only when she had finished for the night and most of the crowd dispersed that we exchanged more than the mechanics that exist between waitress and customer. She was putting on her jacket when I walked up to her.

"You're off?" I asked.

"Yeah. And tired as hell."

"It was pretty busy in here tonight."

"Too busy," she said, undoing her thick, curly hair from the clamp that held it neatly in place and letting it fall against her shoulders.

"Let me walk you to your car," I suggested.

For the next hour or so, Chris and I stood at her car and continued the conversation we had started a few nights earlier. Unlike the last time we had talked, though, there was no longer that strained silence and awkward hesitation. Perhaps this stemmed from my not holding any expectations of what was to follow. Perhaps it was simply the ease that went along with knowing I wasn't trying to get with this woman. I wasn't even trying to screw her. All I was doing was trying to get to know someone I thought might be pretty interesting. And as we stood outside and talked that night, I found that Chris was interesting. She was well-traveled and well-versed in foreign culture and thought. She was mellow and laid back. But most of all, as I mentioned earlier, she was mysterious.

There were bits and pieces of her character that she would show me and then, without warning, shift the pieces around as to suggest another side of who she was. I would later understand after having gotten deeply involved with her that what I initially mistook as mystery was nothing more than evasion. Chris, completely aware of who she was and yet not always comfortable with that person, had grown quite adept at changing faces.

Unfortunately, I wouldn't come to such an understanding until it was too late. But at the time I suppose it really didn't matter. For the intrigue I held toward Chris was equally matched by the emotions I felt for Jackie. I knew what I was doing with Chris, and I knew this had nothing to do with my present relationship. Like I said, it was all background.

By this time Jackie and I had grown pretty close. She had even invited me to attend church with her one Sunday. Though not a very religious man, I quickly agreed, being fully aware of the overtones and implications of doing so. It was keeping in accord with the concept of family and togetherness, something I recognized to be lacking in my own life as well as the lives of so many brothers and sisters.

It also suggested that Jackie was not only willing to take another step with me, but that she too held visions of where she wanted us to be and the path she wanted us to take in getting there. But she and I never made it to morning service. Actually, we never made it too much of anywhere once I began my acquaintance with Chris. It seems that the birth of one thing marked the demise of the other.

"We need to talk," was all she said.

I stared into Jackie's face and tried to define a look she had never shown me before. She kept her dark eyes fixed on me, unblinking, as if she were actually looking straight through me. Her full lips were pursed together in a tense pucker. It was hard to believe these were the same lips I had softly kissed and gently run my tongue over again and again. They no longer invited a warm kiss, but instead seemed cold, hard, and stony. She remained unflinching as she stood posed before me like a chiseled statue. Not knowing what this was all about, and not able to make sense of her odd behavior, I'd hoped to perhaps catch something in her voice that would indicate exactly what was going on.

"Need to talk about what?" I asked.

"We need to talk," she repeated, and then she walked away.

I immediately had that "Shit, what is this about?" feeling come over me. It was ten o'clock in the morning, I had spent the last two hours listening to a classmate read from a manuscript that no one understood, and now this. Trying to ensure myself of my innocence, I began running down the checklist of possible violations I could have committed as I drove home. Had I:

A) Slept with another woman?

B) Been seen on a date with another woman?

C) Tried to talk to her best friend?

D) Lied to her?

E) Screwed her and then ignored her?

My conscious stepped up and assumed the role of commentator. *If you can answer no to all of the above,* it said, *then you have absolutely nothing to worry about.* I ran down the list once more and then emitted five resounding "No's!" As I picked up the phone to call Jackie, I was sure that whatever was wrong must have had something to do solely with her. Maybe she wanted to talk about something going on at home, something with her brother or his wife or her mother or somebody other than myself. But my optimistic twin was promptly bound and gagged by my realistic half. I knew deep down inside that things were much more complicated than that.

Jackie ordinarily did a much better job of listening when it came to our conversations. But the roles were reversed as she picked up the phone and started running her mouth before I could barely identify myself as the caller.

"Hello, Jackie, this is..."

"What we need to talk about," she jumped right in, "is this White woman who works at that Loft you're always going to."

Umm-hmm, I thought to myself, not quite sure if I should say anything at that point or wait and see what came next. Having nothing to hide and wondering what Chris had to do with it all, I chose the former.

"What woman is that? I asked.

"You know what woman I'm talking about. I hear from several people that the other night you stood outside and talked to her for over an hour. They told me how you walked that White woman to her car and was all up in her face smiling and laughing and all this other crazy shit."

This was more serious than I thought. Of the five months I had known Jackie, two of which I had gotten to know her quite well, I had never once heard her curse. Not even a "damn" or "hell." Yet here she was actually "shitting." I didn't say anything as I turned the situation over in my head. Sure, I had walked Chris to her car. So what? It was late at night. I called myself being a gentleman. Sure, we stood outside and talked. So what? I talk to a lot of different people. Was I "all up in her face smiling and laughing?" If there had been reason to smile, I'm sure I smiled. If something funny had been said, I'm sure I laughed. *So what was the problem,* I thought to myself.

Jackie, apparently sensing that I wasn't assuming the openly defensive posture she had anticipated, pressed further with the matter.

"So tell me, Kevin. What's going on with you and this White woman?"

"Her name's Chris," I offered.

"I didn't ask what her damn name was. I asked what was going on with you two."

Jackie was showing me a side of her that I never would have guessed existed. And I didn't like it at all. Yet I wasn't going to judge too quickly. I wasn't going to categorize her as just another insecure sister who felt threatened by a White woman's presence. I wanted to hear her out and find out what could bother her so much that she was making such blind assumptions about what I had been doing behind her back.

"There's nothing going on," I said. "I simply walked her to her car and talked to her for a while. It's the same thing I would have done for any woman leaving work that late at night. You know that, Jackie. You've seen me talking to other women around campus. Why are you now all of a sudden making a big deal out of nothing."

"Because I don't know it's nothing."

"I'm telling you it's nothing."

"Well I don't like it," she said.

"What don't you like? That I was talking to another woman or that I was talking to a White woman?"

"Her color doesn't have anything to do with it," she said. "I just don't want to look like a fool. And that's what this does. It makes me look like a fool."

I wanted to believe her when she said color had

nothing to do with it all. But I knew she was lying. This fault underlying our relationship, which was beginning to divide us like an unsuspecting quake, had everything to do with color. Jackie had seen me on numerous occasions engrossed in conversation with Black women. I'm sure, as it is often a part of my personality, she had even seen me flirting from time to time. But she never said anything to suggest there was an intrusion in our relationship. Only now, only when I'd been seen talking to a White woman, was it automatically assumed that my intentions were anything other than casual conversation.

And it wasn't only Jackie, but the other women who had run back to her like news reporters, must have shared the same belief—the belief that a Black man talking to a White woman was a Black man trying to get with a White woman.

I couldn't help but wonder if such a belief was based more on the image Black women held of Black men, or that of White women. Or did such a belief stem from a deeper truth that suggested a fear within their own selves. Did these women believe Black men were so hung up on White women that surely I was talking to Chris for no other reason than because she was White? Or did they believe White women to be so easy in bed that the conversation must have been a prerequisite to sex?

I wondered further if these were the same women who verbally expressed their bewilderment as to why their men would even be attracted to a straight-hair, flat-butt, bone-thin White woman and yet feared that there was something abut these exact qualities—qualities that Black women do not inherently possess— that had me and my brothers chasing after White women? I couldn't answer those questions. Nor did I think that Jackie could. Not that she didn't know the answers, but that the answers held something I didn't think she was willing to admit. So I didn't press the matter. Instead, I tried to allay whatever fears she may have been harboring at that time.

"Jackie," I said, "I don't know if any of this is because Chris is White or not. You say it's not so I have to accept that. But what I won't accept is your insinuating that I'm out there fucking around. I told you I don't do that. You're the only woman in my life, and you're the only woman I want in my life. As far as Chris goes, well, like I said it was just friendly conversation. Had I known everyone would twist things around and upset you like this, it never would've happened. For that I'm sorry."

Jackie hesitated for a moment before saying anything further. I could almost hear her thoughts being flipped upside down and inside out as she tried to determine whether or not I was being sincere or was I like every other man out there simply trying to get over any way I could.

"Well, I suppose I owe you an apology as well," she said. "I should have come to you and asked what had happened before jumping to conclusions. So I guess in that instance I'm also sorry."

"Listen..." I began.

"But Kevin," she went on. "Don't think for a second that just because I like you that you can do whatever you want and I'm just going to sit around and take it. Because one thing I won't take is being made a fool of. I told you that before. I won't be made a fool of, Kevin."

The words resonated like a bad memory of the past, a memory that takes on true shape and size, steps into the present and threatens to follow us into the future. I thought about Jackie's having been jilted by her fiance and wondered how many other times had she been "made a fool of." I also wondered if she would still regard me as the Kevin she had grown to know or was I once again faced with the formidable task of regaining her trust, my every word and move unjustifiably subjected to deep suspicion.

After hanging up the phone, I lay on my bed for a while staring out the window. It was a cold, dreary morning. The sun made a half attempt at showing itself but was ultimately shadowed by a gray veil stretching across the sky. I thought how senseless it was that Jackie was only fifteen minutes away and yet instead of being at my place and in my arms, she was lying there and I was lying here, our morning having been wasted over what I considered complete nonsense.

Realizing that my lady wasn't going to be there to keep me warm, I went into the kitchen and fixed myself a rich, frothy cappuccino. Then I tossed on a sweater and sat out on the patio. Immersed in the cold air, I found the cup of hot coffee quite soothing in my hands. The little bit of sun that only minutes earlier had tried to come out was now gone. The gray veil had completely taken over and forced its presence onto everything beneath the sky. I took a long swallow of coffee, held the warmth in my mouth and tried to place distance between me and my surroundings. But there was no distance. The veil was over me. It was now only a matter of time before it would touch, embrace and smother me. I sat there as the clouds rolled in and the veil grew thicker. I sat there and waited for the rain to come.

Chapter Five

Chris had decided from the very beginning that it was more than a friendship she was looking to develop. She never came right out and said it, but I suppose she didn't have to. So much of what was between us was suggestion and implication. Talking on the phone with her one night, I realized that, although I knew what I was doing and I had tried to reassure Jackie of this, I had failed to mention to Chris that it was a friend I was in need of rather than a lover. But the posture Chris assumed suggested that her mind was already made up, fixed, and closed.

Not only would Chris not accept that I wasn't physically and emotionally attracted to her, but she didn't even believe it. She had already convinced herself that there was no way I could not be attracted to her. Like so much of American ideology, she must have assumed that her simply being white made her irresistible in the eyes of any Black man. It was inconceivable to Chris that I could talk to her and spend time with her without wanting to seduce her. Not even my admission of being involved with Jackie was enough to convince her of my platonic intentions.

Realizing she was going to believe what she wanted to believe, I didn't bother to waste further time and energy trying to convince her otherwise by mere words. Instead, I set forth over the next two weeks to show her that I was quite sincere in my only trying to establish a friendship with her. We talked on the phone often but never about getting together. There was no innuendo of sexual relations, no words spoken about the possibility of our one day meaning more to each other than we already meant. I had even had her over to my place one afternoon for coffee. That's all it was, and that's all I wanted it to be.

However, Chris had wanted, and I'm sure expected, much more than coffee and conversation. For it was shortly thereafter that her phone calls became less frequent, she became detached, and what I thought was developing into a friendship slowly began to wither and dissipate. Having been shown through my actions that romance was not going to happen with us, Chris was expressing to me through her own actions that she was not willing to settle for my friendship. It was all or nothing.

Quite disappointed that the situation had taken such a turn initially, I also felt a sense of relief that things ended when they did. Although I knew things with me and Chris were innocent, I also knew that Jackie didn't like my talking to her. I therefore couldn't help but feel like I was betraying my lady by going against her desire and doing whatever I wanted. For that, I admit to being very wrong. It should not have mattered that nothing was going on with me and Chris. What mattered was that Jackie had expressed suspicion and discomfort by her presence, and that in itself should have been enough for me to stop associating with her altogether.

Still, there was a part of me that regarded such an attitude as selfishness. Why should I deny myself the opportunity of getting to know other people simply because my girlfriend was uneasy about it? What had I done to give Jackie reasonable cause to question my behavior? Who is she to judge whom I can or cannot befriend?

Posing such questions to myself also forced me to look at myself. In so doing, I realized that it wasn't Jackie who was being selfish, but that it was actually I. Had I been in her place I'm sure I would have felt the same sense of uneasiness she must have felt. More so, it was my blatant disregard for her feelings that rekindled the deep-rooted distrust she had shown me very early in the relationship.

Although we were still together, neither of us could deny that things between us had changed. Communication began to break down completely. My attempts at conversation were often met by a cold silence of indifference. Worse, Jackie often emitted an air that was so inquisitory it lent itself to accusation. The early morning bubble baths and late night massages seemed to have lost the appeal they once held. Candlelight dinners were no longer shared with intimacy, but were instead picked over like a five-year-old admonished to clean her plate. Sex had even gone stale. What was once an expression of true feeling and desire had been reduced to merely going through the motions.

As I tried to talk to her to see if she would actually admit to what was wrong, my question would continually receive the same answer, "There isn't anything wrong." But there was a lot wrong. Jackie, although claiming that everything was okay and that she did in fact still trust me, was exhibiting a behavior that clearly suggested differently. I felt that after several months of trying to get next to this woman, she and I had reverted back to where we'd started. It seemed like nothing I said was right, nothing I did was good enough. Jackie hardly wanted to come over to my place anymore and never wanted to go out. Thinking that we may have needed a change of scenery, I asked her to go away with me to Cancun.

"I don't want to go to Mexico," she said.

"Why not?

"I don't know. I just don't think I'd like it."

A cloud of bewilderment came over me as I tried to understand how my girlfriend could decline such an invitation. Even if it wasn't her ideal vacation, I would think that it was enough that we were at least together regardless of where we went. Had we been in the woods sitting on a rock some place, I still would've enjoyed time spent with Jackie. But apparently she didn't feel the same way about me.

I thought if I told her that my acquaintance with Chris had ended that maybe she would let go of her suspicious fears and I could once again gain her trust.

But I didn't want to bring Chris up. I figured if she hadn't said anything else about it then it was best if I did the same, lest my mentioning Chris actually gave credence to what Jackie was already thinking.

Besides, it was a few days before Thanksgiving and Jackie would be going to New York to spend the holiday with relatives. I thought that since it was obvious she didn't want to vacation with me then maybe it was time apart that she actually needed. Maybe it was what we both needed. A lot had transpired in the last few weeks and I was hoping that the break would give us the needed distance to clear our minds and gain a more objective perspective on where we'd been and where we were headed. That's what I tried to impart to her the day before she left.

"I know things have been a little crazy these past few weeks," I said, "but I don't think this is anything we can't get through if we both still want this. And I want it, Jackie. I want it a lot."

She kept her head turned away from me, her eyes blankly fixed on something across the room. I gently placed my hand beneath her chin and turned her face toward my own. I stared deeply into her brown eyes, silently searching for the emotion she tried to keep hidden.

"Do you still want it?" I asked.

She didn't say anything for a long time as we stood there staring at each other like two strangers from across a crowded room. She then began to slowly nod her head.

"Yes," she whispered. "I still want it."

I softly kissed her on the forehead, pulled her

close to me and, gave her a warm embrace. It was the first time since the Chris confusion had started that she and I held each other like we were still in love and that nothing else around us mattered any more. Had I known it would be the last time we shared such a moment, I would have held Jackie just a little closer, just a little tighter. I would have held her just a little while longer.

Chapter Six

"Dear gracious Lord, we come to you today to say thank you for once again allowing us to sit together and share another meal as a family. We realize just how blessed we are on this day of thanks, but we also realize that there are others who aren't as fortunate as we have been. We ask that you remember those in their time of need and that you provide them the same comfort and strength that you continue to bestow onto us. We thank you, dear Lord, for this food we're about to receive, for the nourishment of our body, for Christ's sake. Amen."

As my grandmother said grace with grace, I sat at the table and thought of all the things in this world for which I should be thankful. I had a college education and worked in a respectable field. I had a few good friends and a very loving and supportive family. I had even been published earlier that year. Yet of all these things, things for which I was truly grateful, it was my relationship with Jackie for which I found myself giving silent thanks on that particular occasion.

I envisioned us a year from the day. We would have Thanksgiving dinner with my family or with her family. Later, as my mind painted a picture much further down the road, we would have our very own Thanksgiving dinner at our very own house with our very own family. Though thankful that Jackie was in my life, I suppose I wasn't altogether satisfied. It wasn't enough to speculate on how things might be in the future. I wanted her by my side right then and there.

Yet it had been three whole days since she'd left town and I hadn't even heard from her. Every time the phone rang, anticipation took over my senses as I longed to hear her familiar voice. But it was always someone else on the other end of the line. It wasn't until Jackie was away from me that I realized just how much I could miss her. But my missing her soon turned to worrying about her as Thanksgiving Day had arrived and still there was no word. I wondered if on the drive up Jackie's brother and wife may have gotten into a heated argument and, in the passion of the moment, careened the van over a cliff or something. *Not likely*, I thought. She was probably just very busy getting reacquainted with distant relatives and hadn't had a chance to call.

With such self-reassurance, I returned to my empty apartment that night expecting to at least find a message waiting for me. But there was no message. It was then that emotion went from missing to worrying to being outright pissed off. What was she trying to prove? Here it is Thanksgiving and she can't even pick up the phone and wish me a good holiday? She didn't even have to catch me at home. A simple "Hi, Kevin, this is Jackie, made it safely, hope you have a nice Thanksgiving, missing you much," would have sufficed. If nothing else, it was common courtesy that went along with being in a relationship.

So was that it, I probed further. Was this Jackie's way of telling me that she no longer wanted to pursue the relationship? Whether or not that was her intention, it was definitely how I took it. It was what I thought and, more so, what I felt. The chasm dividing us was just as deep and just as wide as the distance between New York and Atlanta. The optimism in me wanted to believe that Jackie hadn't called because she wanted to take the time to consider exactly what our relationship meant to her. But I couldn't convince myself of that. The idea that it was only a phone call stood foremost in my mind. It seemed unlikely that she could care enough to continue trying to build a meaningful relationship if she couldn't even pick up the phone and say "hello."

A full week eventually passed and she never bothered to get in touch. I knew then that she wasn't going to get in touch. I also knew that she wasn't going to bring me my cheesecake from Junior's as she had promised.

At that point I had borne witness to several emotions I never imagined I would feel for Jackie. As much as my "distant twin" tried to suppress that other side of me that is capable of feeling softer emotions, I found myself actually hurt by the obvious message she was sending. I only wish that the emotion of hurt was strong enough to mask the anger I felt. But it wasn't. It rarely is.

It was this anger I was acting on when I picked up the phone and invited Stacy over to my apartment. There was no expectation on either of our behalf. No commitment, no strings attached. She knew that I had asked her to come over for no other reason than to get laid. And that was her sole reason for accepting the invitation.

My conscious reared its head as Stacy stood in the middle of my living room and stripped down to her lace bra and thong panties. I tried not to think about Jackie as she slowly moved toward me and pressed her firm breasts into my chest. But how could I not think about her? There I was about to do the exact thing I had promised her and myself I would not do. Yet the mind knows agility quite well, twisting and bending back onto itself until circumstance is how we wish it to be.

It was no different that rainy afternoon as I cursed Jackie in my head for not having called, took a hold of my anger and channeled it in Stacy's direction. The cold November rain dripping down and soaking into the earth seemed to parallel the same coldness I felt inside. In my mixed rage of hurt and anger, I crawled between Stacy's warm thighs and unknowingly forfeited what I thought I had already lost.

Never mind that the sex was good. It was still sex without emotion, a bad habit I had vowed with all intention to kick. It was like doing cocaine. The act itself was an exhilarating, stimulating high. But when it was all over, one sat drained, empty, and depressed. Such was my emotional state as I walked Stacy to the door and mumbled something about, "I'll give you a call" or "we'll get together soon," or one of the many other parting promises that both man and woman recognize and accept as being nothing more than a lie.

Alone once again, I flopped down on my bed and tried to fight off the emptiness by reading a magazine. But it was useless. I went into the other room, grabbed an essay I had been working on and tried to complete it. But I wasn't going to get any writing done that day.

The emptiness shadowed my every move as I stumbled through my apartment either looking for one thing or trying to avoid another. As the emptiness loosened its icy grip and let guilt take a hold of me, I caught myself saying aloud that, "It was just a phone call. All she had to do was pick up the phone and say hello." Still, no matter how loud or how insistent I was at bouncing the words against the wall, the echo always came back the same: "There is no excuse." Deep down inside I knew I was wrong for having slept with Stacy. Even though she was only an old sex partner who had never meant any more to me than just that, it was still wrong.

Sure, my girlfriend had gone out of town over the holidays and failed to call me, but not even that was true basis for doing what I did. Though her not calling suggested things between us were over, Jackie had not actually voiced this to me.

As the affair became a reality that I could not dismiss as easily as I'd done in the past, I questioned my own sincerity toward my relationship with Jackie. Was I ever really in love with her or was it only the idea I loved? Did I actually want her as my future wife or did

I simply want a wife in general? Did she truly play a meaningful role in my life or was she just there to help pass the "in-between" time? I even wondered if I was as mature as I had initially thought, and if maybe I still possessed some of that youthful wildness that makes it so difficult, if not impossible, to make a serious commitment.

Answering such questions required more soul-searching than I was willing to partake in at that time. It had been a long day and an even longer week. So I instead threw on some Sade and poured myself a brandy. The warm drink accompanied by Ms. Adu's soothing lyrics took my senses by the hand and led me to a much quieter place and time. It would be the next morning before I awoke and found myself once again thrust into the center of chaos.

The phone was ringing loud and hard. It had that persistent, mocking tone that suggested it somehow knew I was there.

"Get your ass up!" it screamed. "Get up, get up, get up!"

I stretched across the bed and groped around on the floor until I found the enemy of sleep. With my eyes still half closed and my mind completely closed, I grabbed the cordless phone and slumped back down into the covers.

"Hello," I grunted.

"I'm glad you're there. I was afraid you'd be up and out by now."

The voice on the other end of the line was the same voice I had been waiting to hear for over a week. Even in my state of sleepy confusion I knew exactly who it was.

"How are you?" I said.

"I want to see you. I'll be over in a little bit."

"Wait, hold up."

"What's wrong?" she said.

"Nothing's wrong. It's just that..."

"Don't you want to see me?"

"Yeah, sure, but..."

"But what?"

"It's early, Jackie. It's early and I'm still in bed."

"I'll come get in bed with you," she suggested.

I didn't say anything as I unconsciously began eyeing the sheets on which I had just screwed another woman. There was no way I was about to let Jackie come crawl beneath my covers. I may be an unfaithful, sex-crazed cheat, but I do have some sense of ethics.

"Kevin, is there someone there with you?" she asked.

"No, of course not," I said.

"Then I don't understand why you don't want to see me."

"I didn't say that. It's just..."

"I've been gone for a week," she continued. "I thought you would be happy to see me."

"I do want to see you, Jackie. I've been wanting to see you ever since you left. And I've been wanting to talk to you. But you never called."

"I'll have to tell you about that, Kevin. It was a mess. I'll tell you when I come by."

"Alright," I said wearily, not quite sure if it was the sleep talking or the emotions she had unexpectedly stirred in me.

I pushed the "off" button and dropped the phone

on the floor. I lay staring at the ceiling fan for a while trying to decide what to do next. I only had one set of sheets, so I obviously didn't have time to wash them and remake the bed before Jackie came by. I made a mental note to pick up another set that week, dragged myself to the bathroom and jumped into the shower.

The hot water felt good beating against my tired body. Although I had been in the shower for at least fifteen minutes, I could not seem to get clean enough, could not seem to fully wash away the stains of my moral breach. I softly chuckled to myself as I imagined how Lady Macbeth must have felt.

Time somehow escaped me, for no sooner than I stepped from the bathroom had Jackie begun knocking on my door. Such timing would have ordinarily been perfect. I would meet her at the door wearing nothing but a towel and a hard-on. I would pull her into my apartment and at the same time pull her into my arms. What would happen next? Well, you know.

But I felt as if nothing was perfect that day. If anything, I was annoyed at her having caught me off guard by seemingly sending very mixed messages about where we stood in our relationship. I was certain that she no longer wanted to see me and that what we shared was now dead. And then, like a Phoenix, she became alive again and rose from beneath the charred ruins of spent emotion.

Jackie stepped into my apartment with that same sexy assuredness I first noticed at work. She looked fresh and rejuvenated. I suddenly became self-conscious, wondering if the aura surrounding her could somehow cast a light and expose the dark secret I car-

ried inside. If she noticed, she never intimated anything.

"Give me a hug," she said, opening her arms wide
and inviting me toward her.

I lightly placed my arms around her thin shoulders, gave her a brief hug and quickly pulled away,
realizing that we were standing in the exact spot where
Stacy had stripped half-naked. As I released her from
my arms and stepped backwards slightly, I noticed for
the first time that she was holding a white plastic bag.
"What's that?" I asked, nodding toward the mysterious
package.

"Come on," Jackie said as she grabbed me by the
hand and led me to the kitchen.

She then reached inside the bag and carefully
retrieved a white box with pink stripes. I could tell
immediately that it was a special delivery from Junior's.

"I hope you like cherries," she said. "You never did
say what type you prefer."

She actually remembered to get my cheesecake, I
thought. It had been several years since I'd had what
was often quoted as "New York's Best Cheesecake."
Jalon, a very close friend of mine, had turned me on to
it when we were undergrads. Since then, I've imagined
all of the things I would do for just a slice of the creamy
dessert. And now I actually had a whole cake to myself.
I should have been ecstatic, but I wasn't. I felt like shit.
While I was down here thinking the worst, and then
doing the worst, Jackie was obviously thinking only of
me.

"Thanks a lot," I managed to get out.

"You know, Kevin, I had to go through an awful

lot to get this thing. My cousin lives in Queens and we had to go all the way over to Brooklyn."

"I really appreciate it," I said, hoping she would turn the conversation toward something else.

"And it just added to the confusion and mess we'd had driving up there."

Jackie continued to tell me that her brother and his wife had fought the entire way up. I thought about my initial fear of the van plunging off a cliff and smiled to myself. She went on to confess that she'd thought about me every day that she was gone and that she could not wait to get back.

"So why didn't you call?" I quizzed.

"Well, the cousin whose house we were staying at is really funny like that. He doesn't like for anyone to make long distance phone calls on his phone. Not even family."

"Why didn't you call collect?"

I was amazed that although my own personal fault had more far reaching ramifications than her failure to call me, I still somehow played the role of prosecutor and forced Jackie into taking the defense.

"Well," she said, "I thought about it but figured you probably wouldn't be home anyway. So I just decided to wait until I got back."

She made it all sound so simple. Too simple. Had I not known Jackie, I never would've believed her. But one thing I had learned about her was that she was honest. If there been any other reason for her having not called, she would've certainly said so.

"If the drive up was such a mess," I started, "and things were so hectic, how is it that you manage to look so good and rested and alive?"

She reached out and grabbed both my hands. She then gave me a very warm smile and looked directly into my eyes.

"Because I'm so happy to see you," she said.

I felt sick. My conscious was banging hard against locked doors. It wanted to break free and yell, "I did it! I did it! I'm the guilty party." But Reason quickly stepped in and stood guard to what would have to remain in dark seclusion.

"But enough about me," Jackie said. "Tell me what you've been doing since I was away."

Conscious: I've been fucking.

Reason: Oh, not too much.

Conscious: I had another woman in my bed.

Reason: Just got caught up on some errands.

Conscious: She gave me head in the shower.

Reason: Did a little writing.

Conscious: We fucked here in the kitchen right where you're standing.

Reason: Finished a book I'd been meaning to read.

"Well, you know me," I said. "I did a little this, a little that. Nothing very exciting."

"Let's have some cheesecake," she suggested, "and you can tell me how your Thanksgiving was."

"Sure," I said.

"Let me wash my hands. I'll only be a minute."

Jackie gave me a light kiss on the cheek and then bounced off to the bathroom. It had been a long time since I'd seen her so happy and excited. I thought about the way things were before she left for New

York, the way she had adopted such a cold and distant demeanor. Despite my having just had an affair the day before, Jackie's presence was just as intoxicating as it had been in the beginning. I quickly got over my "sickness," the Stacy incident having been filed away as a meaningless and impulsive mistake that surely would not be repeated. The new found enthusiasm she was expressing about our relationship was contagious. I wanted to make things right again, and I wanted very much to put the whole incident behind me.

But Jackie wasn't about to let me dismiss things so easily. As I leaned against the kitchen counter engrossed in reverie, I felt her eyes boring directly into me. Her stare seemed to snatch me by the arm and pull me back to reality. I looked up and caught her standing at the kitchen door, her once-beautiful face now a Greek mask of tragedy, torture, and throe. It was a grotesque replica of pain itself. I was afraid to ask what was wrong but, strangely, more afraid not to ask. So that's what I did. I asked Jackie what was wrong. She shook her head in bitter disgust and spat the words at me.

"You had that White woman over here, didn't you?"

"What?" I said in genuine confusion.

"You heard me. I said you had that White woman over here. While I was gone, you had her over here and you slept with her."

"What are you talking about?"

Conscious: She knows.

Reason: Impossible.

Conscious: Admit it and get it over with.

Reason: Just stay calm, Kev. Just stay calm.

"Come here," she said, "and I'll show you what I'm talking about."

Jackie disappeared around the corner and stormed down the hallway. I followed like a disobedient child who was about to be spanked and knew it. As she was walking toward the bedroom, I wondered what was back there that could possibly lay claim to my infidelity. Was she going to snatch back my blanket and point an accusing finger at a huge, telling stain? Was there a foreign shade of lipstick smeared on the pillow case? Had she caught the lingering scent of another woman's perfume trapped between the sheets?

Questions raced through my mind seemingly as fast as Jackie ushered me toward the unknown. Yet halfway down the hall she made a sharp right turn and went into the bathroom.

The bathroom, I thought, timidly stepping from the carpet onto the cold tile floor. She was standing a few feet away pointing at what, initially, made no sense at all. On top of the counter next to the sink was a glass jar that I kept filled with condoms. Such was the object of her interest.

"There," she said. "Right there."

"What, Jackie? There what?"

She snatched the jar from the counter and shoved it in my face for closer inspection.

"When I left there was a certain type of condom in here," she said. "I remember. It had a blue package. The only kind like it."

She shook the jar around in an attempt to sort the various-colored "life savers."

"But it's not here," she said. "That condom isn't here."

I knew I said I was attracted to very intelligent women, but, damn, this wasn't exactly what I had in mind. I immediately searched my mental file cabinet of excuses, albeit nothing I pulled out seemed plausible. *I could play dumb*, I thought. Play dumb and hope that she begins to question her own recollection of what was initially in the jar. Or I could claim to have given the condom to one of the fellas living above me as he found himself with a willing woman but no protection. But why bother. My fear was very real that Jackie would reject such nonsense and leave me standing there looking more foolish than I apparently already looked. My fear was even greater that she would actually believe me, leaving me with that sour taste of disrespect I have for a woman so willing to accept what is obviously a lie.

As I turned it all over in my head, I suddenly had a novel idea of actually telling the truth. *That's it, Kev. Just come right out and admit you made a mistake. She's an understanding woman. Surely she can empathize with feeling neglected, abandoned and tossed to the edge of a relationship. After all, hadn't that been her experience so many times in the past?*

"Jackie," I carefully began, "I'm not going to stand here and give you a bunch of bullshit about I didn't do this and I didn't do that. Because I did. I admit I'm guilty."

"Oh, you admit it, huh?" she retorted in a dry tone.

"Some of it."

"What is that supposed to mean?"

"I admit I was with another woman, Jackie. But it wasn't Chris."

She turned her mouth up in a sardonic smile.

"Oh, it wasn't that White woman?"

"No," I said. "It was someone I had once had a little fling with. She's not an old girlfriend or anything like that. Just a sex thing I used to have in the past. It didn't mean anything then and it doesn't mean anything now."

Her smirk grew wider. Even her eyes revealed what she obviously thought of my confession. So strong was her distrust and disbelief that they seemed to take on a true stance of their own, a sense of suffocation crowding itself into the tiny bathroom. How suddenly things had turned around. Only minutes earlier I was in the other room drilling Jackie about her having failed to call me, and now I was the one subjected to humble explanation and apology.

"I'm sorry," I said, and really meant it. "I didn't mean for things to happen this way. It's just that..."

"You must think I'm a damn fool, don't you?"

"What?"

"You heard me. I go out of town for one week. Seven short days. And you turn around and have that White woman in your bed. And there I was actually believing all of that 'I really want this to work, Jackie' and 'I'm really going to miss you while you're gone, Jackie.' I bet I hadn't even crossed the state line and you were breaking your neck dialing that woman's number."

I was embarrassed. Not because I had actually been with another woman, but embarrassed because of the perception Jackie held of me. Not only was it apparent she never truly got past that initial misunderstanding surrounding my acquaintance with Chris, but I now saw that she had already categorized and labeled me as one of those brothers who can't help but lose his mind and his self-control, who can't help but lose himself whenever a White woman came around. The realization was quite clear that Jackie wasn't going to believe anything else I said. She had her own truth to believe.

She continued: "And now you're going to insult me by standing here in my face and telling me that after you've been trying to get with that White woman from the very beginning that she wasn't the one you had over here?"

"Listen, Jackie. I know how this looks and I understand why you think I was with Chris."

She was shaking her head the same way she had done as she stood at the kitchen door, this time expressing further disgust by "um-um-uming" me.

"And you aren't even man enough to admit it," she said.

"Listen, I'm trying to tell you..."

"Kevin, there's nothing you can tell me. It's obvious you would rather be with her than with me. So I'm going to let you do just that. Because I don't want you anymore. I don't trust you and I don't respect you. And I can't be with a man I don't respect."

Jackie calmly walked out of the bathroom and was headed toward the door. I followed her into the living room and then stood in silence as she put on her coat. Ignoring the likelihood of being further reproached, I asked if I could call her later on so that we could talk about it. She stood with her back to me and didn't bother turning around.

"We don't have anything to talk about," she said. "You're always saying how much you want me in your life and how you want us to get even closer and try to build something that's going to last. But how can we build anything, Kevin? How can we grow closer if you can't even keep your dick in your pants for one little week?"

"Jackie..."

"No, Kevin. I don't want you calling me. I don't want to talk to you, I don't want to see you. I don't want to have anything else to do with you."

I didn't know what else to say, not that it mattered. Jackie had already walked out of the door and turned the corner. She wasn't lying when she said she would walk away from a man rather than being made a fool of. I could hear her footsteps hard and deliberate against the wooden stairs, the dull echo a reminder of what I had just lost.

As I held onto the faint sound of her footsteps dying in the distance, it seemed that things with us had also died. But this was not so. For the unrelenting emotions I held for Jackie, and later for Chris, would forever bind the three of us together and breathe life into a small piece of destiny. Jackie's walking away from me that day was certainly a grand exit, stage right. Yet the curtain had not fallen on this play, such events that morning a mere prologue to the ongoing drama that was beginning to unfold.

Chapter Seven

Call it a self-fulfilling prophecy, if you will. Dare even to call it premonition. Either way, I'm sure Jackie must have known that we were doomed from the very beginning. From the first moment I approached her and expressed an interest in getting to know her, Jackie had already begun to expect the worst. And where her expectations stopped, her mother picked up with her constant warning about the way "all men are." As she and her mother were very close, I'm sure Jackie told her everything that had transpired between us, omitting, of course, her own shortcomings in the relationship.

As far as Jackie was concerned, she had no shortcomings, nor did she share any fault in our breakup. Fault only rested in two places: on me and on Chris. Let her tell it, and none of this ever would have happened had Chris not been out to "get me." That's what she'd once said, "That White woman was out to get you all along." Because Jackie never referred to Chris by name, but simply as "that White woman," I wondered what the outcome would have been had she been Black. It's my inclination to believe that her perception of and reaction to the situation would have been markedly different.

My sister and I were discussing this over lunch one afternoon. Munching on her quesadillas, Carmen argued that it made no difference that Chris was White. The only thing that mattered was that I had been with another woman. But I couldn't accept her far-too-logical way of viewing what happened. I was convinced then, and I am convinced now, that had Jackie believed I was sleeping with a Black woman we might still be together. I explained to Jackie that it was a meaningless exchange of sex that was born out of angry, hurt feelings, and I believe she could have accepted that it was something I was truly sorry for having done and that I was sincere in saying that it would not happen again. Although broken trust is a difficult part of a relationship to mend, I know that, over time, I could have shown her that I was once again worthy of her trust and affection.

But Chris was White, and this issue made all the difference in the world. Jackie had shown me long ago just how insecure she was about White women. Though she never came out and admitted how she felt, it was quite obvious that race mattered to her. My alleged affair with Chris thus reached much deeper than the hurt of being cheated on, peeling away her layer of defense and exposing what Jackie not only tried to hide from me, but also from herself. By supposedly sleeping with Chris, my infidelity suggested that it was something far greater that a one-time affair, that this other woman possessed something that she did not and could not ever possess. And how would she possibly compete with that she must have wondered.

Deeply disturbed about the way things had ended with Jackie and me, I called her constantly to see if there was any way I could amend what I had done. I knew that "I'm sorry" meant very little, if anything to her. She'd heard it too many times in the past. But I wanted to show her that I was in fact sorry. I wanted to show her that I realized I had made a mistake and that it was a mistake for which I was willing to pay.

At the same time, however, I didn't feel that the punishment she had cast on me was comparable to the crime I'd committed. My reason for having cheated may not have been justified, but there was a reason. It wasn't as if I just woke up with a hard-on one morning and decided to run out for a quick piece. It was simply a misunderstanding that I grossly mishandled. Put me on a pussy probation for a few weeks. Make me walk her dog, do her laundry, wash her car. But don't toss the relationship away as if it never meant anything.

That was Reason talking. But I couldn't reason with Jackie. For we were looking at the same situation from two very different perspectives. For me, this was all an issue of mistrust. Yet it was much deeper than that from where Jackie stood. Like I said, it wasn't simply a woman, but a White woman, "that" White woman. It was an insult, a spit in the face, a loud shout that "your black ass ain't good enough for me!"

Regardless that none of it was so, it was so in her mind, and she wasn't going to get past it.

So, I spent the next several weeks trying as best I could to get Jackie out of my system. But my memories of her wouldn't go away on sheer will alone. Christmas was right around the corner and the air was thick with the smell and feel of holiday spirit. Couples were holding hands on the street, snuggled all close and warm and cozy. Kids skittered around the stores with that wide-eyed look of anticipation I remember so well from my own childhood. Everywhere I went there was red, green and gold. Colors of festivity, love, peace, and happiness. Yet all I saw was a deep pool of blue swirling up and around me.

I had often read how hard it was for some people to cope with the emotional strain during this time of year. I'd read how high suicide rates climb around Christmas and New Year's, and wondered how things could be so bad during what was supposed to be such a joyous season. But now I no longer wondered how a person could let go and completely give himself to that swirling pool of deep blue. I knew exactly how it could happen.

I was sitting on the floor of my second bedroom. It was supposed to be my library, my study, my writing room. But I'd never gotten around to doing anything with it. Books were strewn over the floor in no identifiable order. Rough drafts of things I'd been working on sat in disarray on top of a round coffee table. My bicycle leaned against the far wall. Yet as disorganized as the room was, it was the perfect spot for gathering my thoughts. It was my think spot. I would sit there at times as though in a trance, turning things over and over in my mind until I had viewed them from every possible angle. That's what I was doing that afternoon. I was turning things over.

I had a large brandy in my left hand and a sharp razor in my right. My eyes were fixed on the stack of Christmas ornaments I'd indifferently tossed into the corner. Jackie was supposed to go with me to pick out a tree. She would help me bring it home and set it up. She would later help me trim it. It was my first Christmas in my new apartment, my first Christmas with my new girlfriend. I had been looking forward to it even before she'd gone to New York. I'd been wanting it. Yet none of this was going to happen, my having thrown it all away over a piece of skinny ass. Of course, Christmas would still come and go. But there would be no tree trimming, no love, peace, and happiness. There would be no Jackie. I would have to spend the holiday alone.

The deep blue was still swirling around me. The more I mulled the situation over, the faster the deep blue swirled, the closer it came. I took a long gulp of brandy, swished it around in my mouth, and then let it slowly slide down the back of my throat. I was holding the razor tightly between my thumb and index finger.

The deep blue.

I lifted the razor over my head and slashed it through the air with violent force.

Deep.

The razor came down hard and landed perfectly.

Blue.

I sliced clean and even, the chunk of cocaine splitting into two perfect halves. I began the task of meticulously chopping the crystalline drug into fine powder and arranging it in several thin lines. It had been at least six years since I'd snorted cocaine. I was a freshman at Howard University, and cocaine was choice. Since then, however, I'd never even had a taste for it, though I'd often been in company where it was passed around freely.

I sat there drinking my brandy and snorting cocaine until my nose was wide open, my senses sharp and alert. The brandy took on a different character. No longer strong and overbearing, the drink was now smooth and fruity, the cocaine having widened my perception of smell and taste. Every now and then I would step outside and get a deep whiff of the cold December air. Someone, somewhere was burning a fire. As the thick aroma of ash and pine floated around me, nostalgia crept in and flashed childhood memories of sitting around the fireplace with my family. I recalled visions of past holidays spent with ex-girlfriends, one girlfriend in particular, and longed to have that warm feeling once again a part of my life.

It can be a very dangerous thing. Nostalgia, that is. It is the stuff from which the deep blue is often made. It gains force and strength through recollection of things past. Each snort took me back just a little further in time, showed me another small piece of my life. The pool of blue grew deeper, grew bluer, and the swirling dared to suck me in.

I can't say for certain how long I was in that room, but now the bottle was only fit for sending a message, and the chunk of cocaine was more than half finished.

I sat there literally out of my mind, dazed in an alcohol and drug-induced stupor. As fucked up as I was, I probably would have snorted every tiny flake of cocaine, let go, and given myself to the swirling blue. But chance would not have it as such. For just as I began to dive deeper and deeper, I heard the phone ringing in the other room.

The same anticipation I felt when Jackie was in New York once again took a hold of me. I even believed in my heart that the call was from her. Somehow, I thought, she had sensed that something wasn't right, that I was slipping away and beyond reach. Even if she wasn't calling to say that she'd forgiven me and that she wanted to give us another chance, simply hearing her voice would have been enough. I climbed down off the walls and staggered to the phone.

"Hello?" I said, trying to sound like myself but knew I didn't.

"Hello, Kev?"

"Yeah."

"How are you?

"I'm fine."

"This is Chris."

Chris, I thought. *What is she doing calling me?* It had been several weeks since we'd last spoken, several weeks since I decided I didn't want to be lovers and she decided she didn't want to be friends. I wondered if she had sensed that I was happily involved with another woman. No way, I thought. *Impossible.* That would make her like some goddamn witch or something. And everybody knows there's no such thing as witches.

As it turned out, Chris said that she was simply calling to see how I'd been doing. She also wanted to know if I was still interested in getting together and going to the market with her. Much earlier during our period of getting to know each other, Chris and I found out that we both have a strong taste for goat meat. She'd gotten turned onto it a few years ago while taking an ethnic foods cooking course. I had my first taste of the succulent meat while in school up at Howard.

There was a small West Indian restaurant a few blocks from campus called Rita's. Although everything there was good, it was at first beef, and later the goat roti that had me coming back time and time again. Yet it had been almost two years since I'd graduated, and my taste for curried goat was now only a memory. But Chris claimed to have a wonderful recipe and even knew where to buy fresh, meaty cuts.

She did most of her shopping at a market near her apartment and had suggested I drive up sometime and we could go together. Of course, I immediately took her up on the offer, already excited about the idea of a large pot of curried goat simmering on my stove. But we never made it to the market, our acquaintance having been truncated by very mixed emotions. I couldn't help but wonder if those emotions were still there, if she had somehow heard that Jackie and I were no longer together and thought it opportune to step up. I didn't know and, frankly, I really didn't care. I was still having major flashbacks of Rita's. With that in mind, I once again took Chris up on her offer.

When's good for you?" she asked.

Definitely not today, I thought. It was going to take

me quite a while to come down off this high, climb out of my hole of depression, and somehow find my way back to a state of normalcy.

"How about Tuesday?" I said.

"Yeah, Tuesday's good for me. I'm off that day."

"Good."

"Let me give you directions to my place," she offered.

"Give them to me later," I said, fully aware that I was in no mental condition to take down directions. "I'll call you before then to make sure we're still on."

"Okay, Kev. I'll talk to you then."

I hung up the phone and stood dazed in the middle of the kitchen. My nose had begun to clog up from the constant draining of mucus into my sinuses. I knew that the only way to prevent my nose from completely closing was to, what else, snort some more dope and blast open the nasal passages. But I didn't want to indulge any longer. My head was spilt wide open, my mouth was dry, my body felt worn and abused. The deep blue was softly lapping back and forth, patiently waiting for me to invite it back. Yet instead, I dumped the rest of the coke and flushed it down the toilet.

I slung my beat-up body across the bed and tried, quite in vain, to get some sleep. I knew the drug would keep me awake much longer than I needed to be. I just lay there staring at the ceiling. I was thinking about Jackie, thinking how she'd been doing, what she'd been doing, who she'd been doing it with. I thought about her accusing me of wanting to get with "that White woman" all along. I never conceded to such feelings, never believed I held such feelings, but it now seemed that the path I was treading, knowingly or not, was definitely headed in that direction. Call it a self-fulfilling prophecy, if you will. Dare even to call it premonition.

Chapter Eight

She was wearing my favorite dress. It was long, very long, all the way down to her ankles long. A deep, rich cranberry, it fastened up the front with ten, twelve,maybe fifteen buttons. Black buttons. She wore it with several undone at the bottom, just enough of a slit to give it a sexy, provocative flare without being overly revealing, without being slutty. That's the way she was. She could take the simplest thing and give it a touch of style and class. Chris was a very attractive, classy lady.

I'd never told her how much I like that dress or how sexy she looked in it. But judging by the way she moved her body and carried herself whenever she wore it, I'm sure she must have known. I'm also sure that's the reason she wore it that day, as we were only going to the market and a pair of jeans would have been just fine. Yet what I would later learn about Chris is that "just fine" usually wasn't enough. Sure, it was okay some of the time. But for the most part she made it her point to go a step beyond "just fine." She made it her point to look good.

Once we finally did get together, that was one of the things I found so attractive about her. No matter where we went or what we did, I never had to worry about any unwanted surprises. She always came to the door wearing the right outfit, her hair nicely done, her face lightly made up. Chris was always looking good.

I often wondered if it was that dress that got me into trouble. As ridiculous as that statement may seem, there's actually quite a bit of reasoning behind it. I once dated a woman for no other reason than the dresses she wore. This was several years ago when I was teaching. Michelle was working at the same school and almost always wore a long dress. She wasn't what one would call an attractive woman, nor was she a very intelligent woman. In fact, a lot of guys would probably call her ugly and dumb. She didn't even flaunt an exceptional body. She was thin, perhaps skinny, and had long, long legs. Model legs. And those legs paired with those long dresses was all it took before I was picking her up and taking her out.

I can't say for certain what it is about long dresses that turn me on the way they do. Maybe it's an attraction to something different. After all, a man—at least this man—can stand only so much skin. But that's the hallmark of women's fashion today. I walk down the street and all I see is cleavage and butt cheeks, midriffs, thighs, and shoulders. It becomes dulling to the senses before long, seeing such open display of one's body leaving nothing to the imagination. I thus find it quite arousing when I see a woman who left the house and actually remembered to put on her clothes.

But this is over-simplifying the matter. And, looking back on what happened with me and Chris, I see nothing at all simple about it. Indeed, things were already beginning to complicate themselves that day at the market. Although Chris and I weren't together, and weren't pretending to be together, I couldn't disregard the sensation that we were, in a subtle, unspoken way, very much together. And this bothered me. The stares bothered me. It seemed that everyone, particularly Black women, kept their eyes fixed on us. Some of the looks seemed to be of curiosity and intrigue, while others unquestionably took on undertones of outright disapproval. It surprised me that in 1992 an interracial couple would draw so much attention. And we weren't even a couple. We were a Black man and a White woman shopping for groceries.

Everyone who watched us with "that look" automatically assumed that we were involved. It was the same mindset I had encountered at The Loft when I walked Chris to her car. But it wasn't only the stares that unnerved me. It was a sensation I couldn't seem to ignore. I thus wondered if my body language, my conversation, the way I looked at and received looks from Chris may have suggested more than was intended. I even questioned whether Jackie's assessment of what was going on may have been more accurate than I wished to believe. Maybe subconsciously, on a deeper level that I kept in suppression, I was really attracted to Chris. It was more likely, I thought, a fear of the attraction that I held, a fear of the possible consequences of becoming attracted to and perhaps falling in love with the exact thing that has supposedly been the downfall of so many of my brothers.

Realization of all things aside, my suggestive personality would inevitably assert itself as I found myself flirting with Chris, found myself flirting with danger. She was bending over looking at some herbs on a bottom shelf. I quietly slipped up behind her and assumed the same posture.

"You better be careful about bending over like that," I whispered in her ear.

Chris stood erect and looked into my eyes. We were standing in the middle of the aisle smiling at each other and exchanging knowing glances. Neither of us said anything, but I think we both could sense that at some point—maybe not that day or the next day or the next day—but at some point one of us was going to say something, and that something would lead us to a place Jackie claimed we had already been.

Having finished with our shopping, Chris and I went back to her place and talked for a while. It was about 7:00 or 8:00 and now dark outside. Every now and then a plane would drift in and out of sight through the large arched window in the sun room. I was sitting on the floor with my back against the sofa. Chris walked over and sat a few feet away.

"Late at night you can see the moon," she said. "It floats across and shines in through the window."

I was staring through the arch into the black sky.

"It's really something," she added. "Almost like magic."

"Hmmm," I softly mused to myself.

We sat in silence and simply stared off into the far distance. It was as if there were expectation in the air. It was as if we were waiting for the moon to crawl into view and show us a piece of that magic. Chris moved a little closer and broke the silence.

"What's wrong, Kev? You look really sad."

I gently bit my bottom lip the way I do whenever I'm considering something. *Was I actually sad,* I thought, *Or was it just those holiday blues doing their thing.* I eyed Chris for a moment as I considered whether it was safe to open up to her. I knew that I was vulnerable, my recent split with Jackie having left much room for another woman to play on or with my emotions. I didn't want Chris to think that my confiding in her was my way of inviting her to step forward and try to fill that empty space Jackie had left open. But I did want to talk about it. I needed to talk about it.

"It's Jackie," I said, my eyes still fixed on the arched window.

Chris didn't say anything but waited for me to continue. I could feel her eyes on me, studying me, the anticipation of what I was about to say like a third party who had joined the conversation and taken its appropriate seat right there on the floor between us.

"I'm not seeing her anymore. She and I broke up."

I shifted my gaze from the window and fixed it on Chris. There was a mixture of concern and hope in her gray eyes.

"I'm sorry," she said, probably damn near about to burst at the seams with excitement.

"You miss her a lot, don't you?" she added.

I slowly nodded yes and then continued to look

out of the window. A train whistle was softly cooing in the still night air. The sound was low and solemn, a reflection of the mood I must have been projecting. The soft whistle reminded me of when I was a kid. There was a train that ran about three miles from house. Yet as far away as this was, I often lay in bed late at night listening to the faint cry. I imagined where the train had been, the many places it had traveled, but mostly where it was going and where it would ultimately end up. Sitting on the floor that night with a strange woman close to my side, my eyes fixed on the night, that sad whistle fading away, I wondered the same thing about myself. Where had I been and where was I going? Chris gently placed her hand on my shoulder.

"Is there anything I can do?" she asked.

"No, there's nothing anyone can do."

"I guess you're right. It's the sort of thing that only time will help you get over."

Well if there was one thing I had it was definitely time. My life after Jackie's departure came to a crashing halt. It was as if she were a big pile of cocaine that I kept my face in everyday that we had been involved. But now the dope was gone, the party was over, and I was coming down off that high fast and hard. Concerned that I was about to get depressed and emotional and all of that shit, I thanked Chris for taking me to the market and told her I should be getting home. She wrote the recipe down and then walked me to the door.

As we stood there in her small foyer, it wasn't long before that sometimes-awkward moment of saying good-bye had sneaked up on us. I had the feeling she wanted me to stay a little while longer, wanted me to say, "You know, as a matter of fact there is something you can do. You can invite me into your bed and help me forget Jackie."

But I didn't say that. I just went home and crawled into my own bed by myself. It was hard and I hated it, hated the emptiness of coming home to a dead quiet apartment and having to go to bed all alone. It was okay during any other time of year, but not now, not when it was so cold outside. I knew I would eventually have to get used to it, for winter was just getting started and the nights would only get colder. By the time Christmas passed and New Year's rolled around, the nights were very cold. I was lying in bed doing what I seem to always be doing: thinking, thinking, thinking. It was a new year, '93, and the first time since I'd been old enough to understand the concept of a New Year's resolution that I hadn't made one.

I recalled previous years when I had, like most people, promised myself things that I knew would never get done. Make a million dollars, cut down on my drinking, stop fucking married women, enroll in graduate school, etc., etc. Yet in '92 I had not only made resolutions that I sincerely believed in, but I had actually attained them. I said I was going to get published and that I was going to fall in love. Both had occurred and both had been as good as I had hoped. But I couldn't say with certainty what I wanted in '93, and that was very unfortunate. Because in the midst of my not knowing, I was ultimately left with whatever came my way. And what came my way was a disaster.

It was early January, January 4th to be exact, and

I had gone over to Chris's to watch a movie. It was a French film. I'd seen the American version, *The Vanishing*, a few years earlier, but the French are more aesthetic in their filmmaking than Americans, and I was very interested in seeing how the original was shot. So that's what I did. I drove up to her place for a movie and conversation.

Unfortunately, I don't remember if the French version of the film was any better than the American. Nor do I remember very much of the conversation. What I do remember, however, is my participation in, and in a sense, initiation of what would become one of the worst and most regretted decisions of my life. Chris was telling me that her back had been hurting lately from leaning over and serving tables at work. She was throwing the bait out, laying it right there on the table, and I took it.

"How about if I rub it out for you," I suggested.

She started playing her coy role again, her role where she seemed to find it unbelievable that all I wanted to do was to relieve her sore back. As I had seen that attitude before, I told her that it was only a massage, that I wasn't asking her to take off her clothes.

"Actually," she said, "I would feel a whole lot better if you were asking me to take them off."

Ding! Ding! Ding! Ding! Ding! Red Alert! Red Alert! Warning signs were going off like crazy. Lights flashed. Bells rang. Railroad crossbars came down and warned "Caution. Caution. Do not cross to the other side. I repeat, do not cross to the other side." But I didn't heed any of it. My mind was already obscured by stepping into a new year, by stepping into Chris's place, with no true sense of focus or direction, no idea of what I was pursing. And the man who doesn't know what he is pursuing ultimately becomes the pursued.

Thus it was on that cold winter night that I made the grave mistake of climbing into Chris's bed. For in the process of stripping away my clothes, I was also stripping away a small piece of myself. And that part of myself that I did not willingly shed, Chris would later, without mercy and without apology, suck from me.

Chapter Nine

"I've been wanting to do this for a very long time,"she whispered.

I couldn't see her as she spoke the words. Her face was a mere silhouette in half darkness. She was there, but not there, like a fleeting image that surreptitiously comes in the night and is no more. It had the feel of a deceptive dream, a dream that distorts one's ability to distinguish the imagined from the actual. Music was playing in the background, yet the voice crooning from my stereo suddenly became dull and insignificant. It was only her voice I could hear, only her words that held true meaning.

Not knowing how else to respond, I placed my hand on the back of her neck and pulled her close to me. Her words were still echoing in my mind: "I've been wanting to do this for a very long time." And then she did it. As if the act came as natural as breathing itself, Chris wrapped her soft hand around my hard sex and gave me some of the best head of my life.

I remember the night quite well. It was Super Bowl Sunday, and Chris and I, having grown bored with the game, sat around listening to music, drinking beer, and talking. Although it was our fourth time getting together, we still had not gone out and actually done anything. That's how it was in the beginning. She was either at my place or I was at hers. We weren't doing the customary dating thing; we simply "got together" and spent some time. Although I was a little uneasy with this arrangement, for I was still quite sincere in my trying to stay away from casual sexual relations, I tried to convince myself that things were very early and that we were still feeling each other out. And so I let it go, and I let it go.

Before I knew it, she and I had been seeing each other for several weeks and still there had not been one play seen, one dinner shared, one walk through the park. All we did was screw. Regardless that the sex was good, in fact was very good, it wasn't at all what I was looking for. This was particularly so after everything that happened with Jackie. There was no way I could've accepted my having thrown away something of true meaning and substance for an exchange of empty physical pleasure.

As nothing was seemingly headed toward change and we stepped into our third week, my concern grew into a fear I had never before known. *Am I*, I found myself asking, *one of these brothers who unknowingly have bought into the myth surrounding White women and their very liberated exploits in the bedroom?* And further, my fear forced me to question, *had Chris*

bought into the same myth concerning Black men's sex-
ual prowess and thus relegated me to a position only fit
for the bedroom? Not willing to accept either stereo-
type, I was determined to dispel the idea that I was
with Chris only because she gave excellent head or that
she herself considered me nothing more than a good
lay.

We were lying in bed one morning when I rolled
over and asked her if that was indeed how she felt
about me and the time we spent.

"What...do...you...mean?" she yawned, a hot wave
of fetid morning breath blowing all in my face.

"Exactly what I said. Is this just a sex thing we got
going on here or what?"

"Not for me. Why? Is that how you feel?"

"You know that's not how I feel," I said. "I've told
you before how I feel."

"I feel the same way, Kev. I'm twenty-two years
old. I'm not out running around looking to spend a little time here, a little time there. I did all of that when I
didn't know anything else. But that's not what I want
right now. That's not what I need."

"What do you need?"

"The same thing you need. Something real in my
life."

I've learned that there are two types of people
when it comes to trust. Some individuals trust blindly
until they have reason not to trust. Others trust no one
until trust has been gained. I've always subscribed to
the latter philosophy. But on that morning I swayed
from such doctrine. First of all, I wanted very much to
believe Chris. I wasn't prepared to admit to myself that

our getting together had been a big mistake. And secondly, tucked deep down in the covers and snuggled next to a pretty, warm woman on a bitter cold morning, I found it very, very easy to believe.

"Then let's get out of bed and go do something later on," I suggested.

"Fine," was her response.

So that's what we did. We got up that day and for the first time took our relationship beyond the confines of my apartment. Ironically, however, I don't recall how we spent what would become our first "date." Yet the sex that followed later on that night remains a vivid image in my mind. Conversations we held, funny incidents we experienced, the nights out we shared would, from time to time, escape me. But the sex never did. I always remembered the sex.

So too would I always remember those words: "I've been wanting to do this for a very long time." Chris hadn't known me for that long—didn't really know me at all—and yet she was willing, desiring, to share an intimacy that some women don't even share with their husbands. When asked why she was so quick to do what so many other women had to be coaxed, begged, threatened, or even paid for doing, her response was as simple as most things were in her life; "Because I like doing it and it turns me on." And I admit that to know it turned her on turned me on as well. But the dynamics of Chris's oral tendencies, as I would later understand, were much larger than sheer sexual desire. They had, in fact, more to do with her sense of self and how that helped form her role in our relationship.

Despite Chris's propensity to evade so much of what was around her, one thing she made very clear to me was that she was not only willing, but that she actually preferred and needed, to play a subservient role to her man. Extremely passive by nature, Chris's oral performance was a symbolic gesture akin to bowing down at the altar and paying homage to a demigod.

Before she and I took time to establish a relationship, or even a true friendship, Chris had already defined the parameters of our existence together. She needed her man to keep her subjected to a background position, and it was my role to do just that. *To do otherwise*, I told myself, *would be remiss in my duties.* So I willingly played the role she cast me in and kept Chris on her knees.

Accustomed to the unyielding strength of Black women, I initially found Chris' passive, easy–going nature quite refreshing. I couldn't help but compare her to Jackie. I remember how I not only had to ask Jackie to perform for the first time, but that I had to ask for such attention every subsequent time. And though she was always willing to go down—willing because it pleased me, not her—she approached it with an air that implied I was degrading, even punishing, her. It was a chore to Jackie. And this was no turn-on. I mean, how aroused can a man get when his lady is going down with a sick, grotesque look on her face?

Not only the oral practice, but sex in its entirety with Chris shared dominant/subservient overtones. Not once would she ask me to "make love" to her. But she was quick to tell me to "fuck" her. The only other women who had phrased themselves so bluntly with me were casual partners wherein we both understood that that was all we were doing—we were "fucking."

The connotations carried a sense of being detached, transient, perhaps even dirty. Still, even I, a writer and former English teacher, had learned to look beyond semantics and extract a sense of perverse eroticism from it all.

What should have otherwise been an act of closeness and gentle intimacy was thus expressed very roughly with me and Chris. Our sex at times seemed almost abusive. We were on my living room floor one day doing our usual thing when I found myself grabbing her thick curly hair and pulling on it as one would the reins around a horse's neck. The harder I pulled, the more she enjoyed it. If I weren't trying to pull her hair out by the roots, I was often leaving red palm prints on her white ass from the harsh spankings that gave her so much pleasure.

We would sometimes find dark bruises on her arms and legs—neither of us actually recalling how they got there—as a reminder of just how rough our sex could become. Thinking back on the many times we laughed and joked and had so much fun together, it seems Chris was never quite as content, never quite as happy, as when she left my place with, as she endearingly phrased it, a "sore and swollen pussy."

Though she and I had gotten to a stage where we often went out and shared things other than sex, it seemed, not only with her but with me as well, that the sex following our outdoors activity was always the anticipated part of our having gotten together in the first place. It was as if our going to the theatre or the park or the coffee house or shopping or whatever was a mere facade of what we both knew, yet never admitted, was the premise of our spending time together. Sensing that aching fear creeping out of the closet I never seemed to shut tightly enough, one day I asked her if she would continue seeing me if we weren't sleeping together. Her answer was an emphatic "No!"

"Then is that all I'm good for, Chris? Is to fuck you?" I said.

"It's not that, Kev. It's just that I like you. I like you a lot. But I like all of you. Not just your conversation or your mind or your personality. But I like all of Kev, and I want all of Kev. And that includes sex."

It should have been obvious that, although our relationship had grown to encompass constructive activity away from the bedroom, it was still there, in between the sheets, that we had defined our relation toward one another. But I would not believe it, could not believe it. For to believe it would be to breathe life into my fear that I was nothing but her Black stable boy on call to keep her stuff "sore and swollen," and that she, in turn, was just my White whore willing to wear out her knees at the altar. So I didn't believe it. I instead whipped out the demigod and let her make her offering.

Chapter Ten

I was only eleven years old when my mother passed away. Yet I remember her well. I remember her face, her large smile and robust laughter. But mostly I remember her words. A very strong woman, my mother tried to instill this same strength in me as a child. She would often say that I could do anything I wanted if I set my mind to it and that my foremost responsibility in this world was to myself. "But you have to be true to yourself," she softly advised. "You have to be true to yourself." As if the words were a foreshadowing of so such to follow, my mother gently let go of my hand as she lay in bed encouraging me to leave her side, lest I be late for school. She died that very same day.

Although my mother would no longer be a part of my physical life, her words have always remained close to me. Never haunting, the advice has served as a sort of maxim to the way I approach my world around me.

For so many years I've believed in and lived by those very words. It wasn't until Chris came into my life that I began straying from what before was such a constant.

The first time that I realized I was ignoring my mother's advice was when I should have walked away from the relationship and never looked back. Chris and I had been going out for almost two months when it happened.

I was taking my trash to the dumpster one day when I saw three people coming down the stairs of a nearby building. The group was comprised of a Black man, a White woman close at his heels, and a Black woman pulling up the rear. Of course, I knew absolutely nothing about these people, had never seen them before in my life.

But seeing them that one time was all it took before I was making judgment.

I watched the three as they proceeded across the parking lot and approached a parked car. The man then opened the front passenger door and let the blonde step in.

Once assured that she was safe and snug, he shut the door and walked around to the driver's side, leaving the Black woman to fend for herself. Although it was the middle of February and biting cold outside, I began to feel that hot, sticky sensation crawling over my skin. My face turned twisted and sour. My lips puckered as if having tasted something foul. I was annoyed, disgusted, incensed. I was mad as hell. Granted, I wasn't aware of the circumstance surrounding what I had just seen. I had no idea what personal or nonpersonal relations may have existed between the three of them. But it didn't matter. All that mattered was my perception of the scene and its subsequent implication.

It was at that moment that I realized I was doing the exact same thing people had done when seeing me with Chris. I was stereotyping, making judgment without the facts. Still, I know what I saw and what I felt. And it wasn't good at all. I was pissed off that one of my brothers would publicly display such obvious disrespect for a Black woman. But it wasn't the anger that bothered me most. Rather, it was that disturbing reality that often comes with viewing one's self. One can't lie his way around it. He can't deceive it. For no matter how cleverly he creeps up to the looking glass and tries to steal a glance, his reflection always catches his eye, always stares him right back in the face.

A stranger who happened to pass through my life for no more than a brief moment, that man was certainly my very own reflection. That man was I. For despite having seen what I'd just seen and having felt what I'd just felt, I jumped in my car and followed suit. It was only a few minutes later that I was flying down I–20 breaking the speed limit, breaking the law, all just to see my very own White girlfriend.

"You have to be true to yourself."

The words were as loud as church bells. But I wasn't being true to myself. I was lying to myself and I was cheating myself. By doing otherwise I knew that I would have to face and admit too much of what I felt. I didn't want to believe that another person's race made a difference in the way I perceived her. I didn't want to believe that like so many of us in this society I still, all lip-smacking rhetoric aside, was not comfortable with interracial relationships.

Indeed, I recall several engaging conversations I've had in the past in which I claimed to be indifferent to it all. I'm sure you know how it goes. "Hey, if two people really care about each other then that's their business." And I believed that—believed it, that is, until it actually touched me.

Still trying to appease a guilty conscious, I told myself that my reaction to what I'd seen in the parking lot that day was different. It wasn't about an interracial couple, I said. It was about disrespect. Open, blatant disrespect. But the facade was too thin to hide true feelings. As Chris and I began spending more time together and venturing into the scrutinizing public eye, I was not only forced to acknowledge those feelings I'd tried to pretend did not exist, but I also experienced feelings I had not known were there.

Though I had obviously seen interracial couples before Chris and I started dating, it was only after my crossing to the other side that I noticed them with a more watchful eye. Surprisingly, I caught myself staring whenever I passed a White woman wrapped in the arms of a Black man. This was usually the case when I was alone and particularly so when Chris was by my side. More unnerving, almost to the point of being creepy, was the exchanged look I would share with one of my brothers as we approached each other on the sidewalk like two reflections, two long, dark shadows that we could not seem to shake loose.

It is a peculiar thing the way Black men greet each other when passing, the way we throw up our heads in a sort of reverse nod. But these greetings were much different. Like I said, it was creepy. It had the eerie sensation of meeting one's Doppleganger for the very first time. I look into his dark eyes and try with all naturalness to give him that symbolic heads up as I mouth the words "what's up?" Yet it never comes across as natural and genuine. On the contrary, it's actually quite contrived. For the scary thing about our meeting is that we both know quite well, too well, what is up. I see it in his eyes and he sees it in my eyes. And I wonder if the women on our arms, these two White women, also share an all-knowing and unspoken exchange, an exchange far scarier than anything I've ever known.

Of course such exchanges weren't nearly as frequent as the exchanged stares Chris and I received whenever we were out. But a stare isn't simply a stare. There was suggestion and connotation accompanying every look.

White men unquestionably wore a look of bitter rage. "How dare that dirty nigger defile such a pure and innocent White woman!" their eyes seemed to scream. And a part of me, I must confess, received a strange sense of satisfaction from it all. Yet it had nothing to do with the "forbidden fruit" concept that is often posed as one of many reasons Black men pursue White women. Instead, it shared a closer resemblance to a twisted and irrational form of receiving psychological reparation. Each time Chris would go down on me, each time I thrust deep and hard into her "sore and swollen pussy," each time my black hand came down and smacked her white ass, that small piece would seemingly yell in fulfilled ecstasy, "This is for that day you asked to see my

I.D. without probable cause." Bap! Bap! Bap! "This is for every time you've called somebody a nigger." Bap! Bap! Bap!

I would then roll over and lie next to Chris just as mentally exhausted as I was physically, that small, twisted piece snickering in the recesses of my mind, "*That* is how I defile such a pure and innocent White woman."

I wish I could admit to also finding satisfaction in the cold, cutting stares that Black women would cast my way. But these stares held much more meaning than those of White men. The young women, those whom I could very well had been dating, looked at me as though I had personally offended and betrayed them. The stony canvas of their faces and the penetrating glare in their eyes asked me in all earnest, What was this White woman doing for me that they themselves could not do? What type of spell had this stranger cast over me that had me overlooking all of the single, attractive, educated Black women in Atlanta? And of course I didn't have the answer. Not for them, not for myself. I would simply look the other way and write it off as just a bunch of angry sisters who didn't know how to keep a man.

Such quick dismissal may have worked when averting the intense stares of young women, but my Conscious was never able to combat the look older women threw my way. When I say older, I mean old enough to be my mother, some of them even my grandmother. Because of such a vast age difference, it was obvious that these women weren't saying to themselves, "Damn, there goes another brother I have to strike off my list." No, that would've been far too easy for me to handle. Instead, it was a softer look, a look of deep concern. It was a very maternal look that reminded me so much of my mother and those words she gave me to live by.

I remember one morning Chris and I were out having breakfast. Everything was going fine. The food was good, conversation was good. She and I were laughing a lot that morning, as the night before had been very nice and left the two of us with what I hope remain fond memories. But this all changed very quickly as an older Black couple was seated directly next to us. They looked to be in their late forties, early fifties, I guess. The man doesn't come clearly to mind. He simply sat down and immediately stuck his nose in the menu. His hungry ass didn't even look our way, I don't think. But that woman—oh that woman.

As the tables were placed very close together, I could have reached right over and touched her with my arm still slightly bent. So close were we that I could feel the tension rising and swelling like a puffy rain cloud that's about to burst open and let go of everything inside. I thought she was actually going to say something, but she didn't. Yet I wish she had. Like I said, I could've dealt with that a lot easier. But she did what I feared most. She looked over at us, gave me a woeful look of despair and slowly shook her head back and forth. I even heard her whisper "God bless you."

Chris never noticed any of it. She merely kept her eyes fixed on the stack of pancakes she was carefully cutting. And that's probably where they would have remained had I not half–dropped, half–tossed my fork onto my plate, the distinct clink-clank of stainless steel against China enough to cause several heads to turn our way. It seemed that a hundred pairs of eyes were staring from nameless, blank faces, their round lips silently mouthing the words "You have to be true to yourself." Yet at that moment I felt as if there were no such thing as truth, as if everyone in the restaurant had been caught on canvas by the fiercely imaginative stroke of a surrealist painter.

"What's wrong?" Chris asked as she looked up and saw the bizarre mask I must have been wearing. "Kev, what is it?"

There was a slight touch of uneasiness in her voice.

"Nothing," I said. "I just lost my appetite, that's all. I just lost my appetite."

Before it was all over, I would lose a lot more than my appetite. I would lose my direction, sensibility and emotion. I would lose myself. But this was a slow, gradual, wearing away process, like the constant running of water over rock until, seemingly overnight, it cracks and splits open, the water cutting a deep grove and claiming it as its very own. I could feel that something was wearing on me the same way, that something was lightly tugging at the seams which held me together. Thinking my feelings were the result of having grown so conscious of race, one night I raised this concern with Chris.

She was at my place late one night. As my apartment was only a few blocks from The Loft, she would often pack an overnight bag and come by when she got off. I really enjoyed those late night visits. Having always been a night person, I found it strangely appealing to have a visitor softly rapping on my door at the witching hour. Such visits were uneventful but nonetheless very intimate. She and I would usually sit around and share a drink or two as we talked about what we had done that day or what we were doing the next day or just about anything. It was never anything too serious; just very light conversation.

Sometimes we would make love or fuck or do whatever it was we were doing. But this usually waited until the morning. Chris would come by and jump right in the shower. I would often already be lying in bed with a glass of wine. She would then crawl beneath the sheets, her body soft and warm, and we would lie there and enjoy each other's company until we drifted off to sleep. Nights like that were good. They were very good.

This one night, however, things just didn't go the way they had been going. It was 1:00 or 2:00 in the morning. She and I were sitting around eating pizza and drinking white Bordeaux. As usual, conversation was confined to this, that, and the other thing. That's when I swiveled around on my bar stool and looked at her.

"You know, Chris," I began, "you and I have been going out for almost two months now and we've not once discussed the issue of race."

The word seemed exceptionally heavy coming off my tongue. There are some words that roll off the tongue. Others may leap forward, seductively slide out or crawl into the air. But that word, "race," seemed to fall out of my mouth like a heavy weight. I could feel

the tense uneasiness in the room. It was Chris's uneasiness, the same uneasiness I had detected in her voice
that morning at breakfast. She didn't say anything for a
while as she carefully picked the mushrooms from her
pizza.

"I think that's pretty strange," I eventually said.

"What's strange about it?"

"Well, I mean, here we are an interracial couple
and..."

"Yeah? So what?"

"I just find it strange that the issue of race has
never come up between us." Chris let out a weary sigh
as if not wanting to be bothered with any of it.

"I suppose it's never come up because it's not an
issue with me," she said.

"What do you mean it's not an issue? How can it
not be an issue?"

"Because I don't look at you and see a Black man,
Kev. I look at you and I see a person. That's how I
think of you and that's how I treat you. As a person."

I was slowly swirling the wine around in my glass
as I considered everything she was saying. Having
removed all of the offensive mushrooms, she placed
her finger in her mouth and lightly licked the tomato
sauce. Chris then turned and looked at me.

"Why, Kev? Is it an issue with you?"

"Of course it's an issue," I said. "It can't help but
be an issue."

"So I suppose when you look at me all you see is
a White woman, huh?"

"Well, Chris, you're obviously White."

And she was. Not bronze or tan or cream, but

white. Very white with gray eyes and thick, curly hair. Her faith was Protestant and her blood was German. No, there was no mistaking her for anything other than white.

"It's not that I look at you and see only a White woman," I said. "And I hope you mean it when you say you don't simply see me as a Black man."

"I do mean it."

"But I am a Black man, Chris. I'm a young, educated, Black man in America.

Race has to be an issue to me. It's an issue to me because it's an issue to this society. Add to that the reality that I'm fucking a White woman and it becomes even more of an issue."

The lighting in my apartment was low and subdued, yet I could still see the exasperation in those gray, cat-like eyes. She was bored with and indifferent to that for which I held such strong conviction. She was probably wishing we could go back to discussing the newly-released CD or the upcoming movie or whatever insignificant shit it was we were talking about before I got so serious.

"I'm sorry," she said. "I wish it was an issue to me but it just isn't. It wasn't an issue in my house while I was growing up, it wasn't an issue after I got older and moved out, and it's not an issue to me now."

Where had I heard that before, I was thinking to myself. "It wasn't an issue in my house." The words were strikingly familiar. I tried to recall who it was I had heard say that, what talk show, book or magazine I'd first been exposed to such a claim.

"It was never an issue with my parents or my

friends or the men I dated."

The familiarity of her claim grew louder and nearer though her voice and position had not changed.

"I don't associate with people who are all hung up on race, Kev. I don't waste my time with any of that because I don't want it around me. I don't want it in my life."

It finally reared its head and showed me the common, familiar face I knew I had seen before. "Kev," she said, probably with true sincerity in her heart, "I'm not like most White people."

Ahhah! That was it. It wasn't anything I had heard any one specific person say. It wasn't splashed across the cover of the newspaper or featured in one of the weeklies. It was, quite simply, a self-deluding, self-appeasing attitude adopted by the mass majority of White America. It's like the neighbor down the street who claims not to be a racist, who invites a Black person over for lunch or tea, but who then automatically assumes when hearing of a horrendous crime that it must have been committed by an out-of control Black man.

I'm sure Chris really did believe she stood apart from most of her people. And I wanted to believe it, too. Because to believe that every White person in America shared the same distorted, crippling mindset was to concede that this country is in more disarray than we already know it to be. And I didn't want to take such a pessimistic stance. So I gave Chris the benefit of the doubt until she showed me otherwise.

"Look..." I said.

"Kev, it's late. Okay? I've been at work dealing

with those people and I'm tired. The last thing I want to do is sit here in the middle of the night having some heavy conversation about race."

"Alright, Chris. I'll leave it alone."

She wrapped her arms around me and buried her face in my neck.

"All I want to do is get in bed with my man and go to sleep."

Yes, of course, I thought. The bed. Every path we took, no matter what direction, up or down, straight or winding, always led us back to where we had started. We hadn't even been under the sheets for ten minutes before I heard the steady, rhythmic breathing of hard sleep. Just that quickly and easily Chris had dismissed everything I said and slipped off into her own little world. I lay there with my back to her. She was pressed into me with her right arm slung over my side, one of her legs intertwined with my leg, her breath hot and heavy on my neck. She had obviously found her spot and nestled into it with much content. I was staring at the red lights on my clock as they stared back, 3:11, 3:12, 3:13...

The bright numbers eventually faded to a fuzzy haze as I slowly fell asleep. It was a deep, troubled sleep, the kind of sleep I had when my mother was sick and dying. I remember praying to God each night to please let her live. He had already taken my father, and my childish mind thought that one parent should have been enough. But it wasn't enough. He snatched my mother from me and in exchange gave me horrendous nightmares that never seem to go away. At best they only flee into remission, giving my heart and mind temporary solace every now and then. That's where they had been until that night. They were in remission and my soul was at peace. But I knew they would eventually return. They always did. As I drifted off to sleep that night, those childhood nightmares awoke loud, angry and screaming. They awoke with a vengeance.

Chapter Eleven

It was going to be a good concert. George Duke, Howard Hewitt, Diane Reeves, George Howard. A night of jazz at the "fabulous Fox Theatre." That's how every show was advertised that came to the Fox. It was purported to be fabulous. And they usually were. The theatre was large, grand, and historical. It claimed and held onto a piece of time that gave it a special, almost noble, air of dignity.

I knew it would be a very memorable evening. Having heard of the show perhaps the first day it was announced to the public, I quickly purchased two of the best seats in the house. The view from the luge was spectacular, the music crystal clear. It was being held the night after Chris's birthday. She had a strong fondness for jazz and had even turned me onto a few things to add to my own collection.

I bought the tickets at least a month in advance with the intention of our still being together by the time her birthday rolled around. But within that very short period of thirty days, something had changed.

I was talking to my grandmother about the show and, upon mentioning that it was Chris's birthday, she said in a mixed tone of coincidental irony, "That's Barbara's birthday." More so than mere coincidence, the fact that my mother and my girlfriend shared the same birthday made me consider those words even more closely. "You have to be true to yourself."

Not until I was reminded of my mother's birthday did I consider how she would have felt had she been alive to see what her son was doing. I wanted to believe that it would not matter to her, that because I was her son and she loved and accepted me for who I was and the decisions I made, that she would also accept the woman I had chosen to make a part of my life. But my mother was the same lady who had worn little White girl's hand-me-downs that my grandmother brought home from the houses she cleaned for a living. She was the same lady who was subjected to the violent and hateful discrimination of the segregated South. She was the same lady who was constantly told that she was less than a White woman simply because.

The more I thought about my mother and my relationship with Chris, the more ashamed I became. I felt that my mother would also be ashamed and that she would, like that woman I encountered at breakfast, shake her head with the same look of disappointment in her eyes and wonder what was so wrong in my life that made me stray so far away from everything she had instilled in me.

As Chris's birthday grew closer, I could see that

she was really looking forward to the evening. She had shown me the dress she was planning to wear and solicited my opinion about a pair of Kenneth Cole pumps she wanted to buy just for the occasion. But she didn't need my opinion. The dress was gorgeous and the shoes were sharp as hell. Chris had very good taste in clothes and she knew it. No doubt, I would have stepped into the Fox that night with a very fine lady on my arm. But it was a White lady, and the reality of it all sat before me larger than that big old theatre itself.

The irony did not escape me that it was initially I who expressed concern about Chris and I keeping our relationship in the closet, and yet once we did begin to spend time together in public I was the one who could not handle it. I thought that it wouldn't bother me, but it did. That was the lie I had been living.

It was only a few days before Chris's birthday that I knew there was no way in hell I could walk up into a function with so many brothers and sisters while hugged all up on a White woman. As my feelings of shame and betrayal slowly ate at my psyche like a cancerous tumor, I told myself that I wasn't a sellout for taking Chris to the show, but that, conversely, my not taking her was selling out. I was selling out myself, as I realized that I had allowed what others perceived of me and my relationship to push me away from Chris. Yet this was a woman I claimed to care about, a woman I enjoyed spending time with, a woman I thought I could love. It was no one's business but my own if I wanted to date a White woman. Still, regardless how much I tried to psych myself up, those words, "you have to be true to yourself," took a hold of my mind and my heart and simply would not let go.

As much as I knew it would hurt Chris for me to walk away from the relationship, especially on such a special occasion as her birthday, there was no way I could forfeit my own sanity and inner peace all in an effort to make her happy. So I called it quits. I didn't take her to the show, I didn't buy her a present, I didn't even send her a card. I instead went to the cemetery that day and placed fresh flowers on my mother's grave.

Chapter Twelve

It is an unbearable feeling to love someone you know you could never have. It is even more unbearable to love someone you don't want. I hesitate to say that I actually loved Chris after only two months together, but I did hold very real feelings for her. I cared about Chris a lot and hated that the only way I knew how to handle so many agonizing emotions I felt inside was to walk away and hurt her. In doing so, however, I found that Chris wasn't the only one who was hurt by my decision. I too was torn apart after having said good-bye.

The week following Chris's birthday was an attestation to just how paradoxical my feelings and attitude were concerning the relationship. I liked Chris. I liked the way she made me feel, the way we laughed together and had so much fun. I liked going to bed with her wrapped in my arms and then waking up to find her still pressed firmly next to me. And of course I liked the sex. Still, none of this could negate those feelings of guilt and shame that kept staring me in the face.

My body literally ached after having turned my back on it all. As I thought about some of the things we had shared and experienced together, my mouth would become dry, the pit of my stomach sick and queasy. It was similar to those feelings I had after Jackie walked out of my life, but much more intense. More intense because it had been my decision to throw away what at times was so good, more intense because the problem actually had nothing to do with the other person. It was a psychological and emotional dilemma that I myself carried around. As such, removing myself from the relationship wasn't enough. It was the Demons inside that were tearing me apart, and it was those Demons I would have to confront if I hoped to have peace of mind and soul.

I called Chris a week later. It was a beautiful spring Saturday in Atlanta and that special feeling was in the air. I don't know where I found the presumption to call her. I had done the unspeakable; I had dumped a woman on her birthday. But at that point, after the ache of having gone a week without hearing her voice, without seeing her face, without having her close at my side, it all seemed insignificant. Yet I wasn't calling with any real expectation in mind. I simply wanted to talk to her. I needed to talk to her.

Chris answered the phone and tried to sound just as casual as always. But I could hear the apprehension and suspicion in her voice. I could hear the hurt in her voice. She said that her birthday had been nice despite everything, that her friends had taken her out and refused to let our breakup get her down. I was really glad to hear that, as I still felt awful for having committed such an irreparable act. Though what I would find out is that it wasn't as irreparable as I had thought, and that the myth that White women are much more tolerant than Black women wasn't a myth at all. It became very clear to me that Chris was willing to excuse such things the thought of which a sister wouldn't even entertain.

"I want to see you," I said, almost as if nothing had ever happened.

"Why?"

"I don't know, Chris. I just do."

Silence crept in between us and seemed to echo the emptiness I had felt over the past week. She then said, "Where do you want to see me?"

"I thought I would drive up. We could talk for a little while. That's all. Just talk."

"What do you want to talk about, Kev?"

"I don't know, Chris. I just want to talk."

That silence returned as we both must have been considering the same thing. With our breakup being so recent, and with so many emotions still involved, I wasn't sure if being in each other's presence may have actually made things more difficult.

"But if you think it's best that I don't come by," I said, "then of course I'll understand."

"No it's okay. I'll be fine."

"So I'll see you in a little bit?"

"Okay, Kev. I'll be here."

The drive up I–20 seemed exceptionally long that afternoon. As the radio in my '78 Celica was on strike that day, my mind had no choice but to listen to itself. What was I hoping to gain by going over to this woman's house, I asked myself over and over. *You already saw that being with a White woman was too much trouble, that it created too much of an inner turmoil. You know you're just asking for more trouble, Kev. You know you are. So why is your dumb ass driving up there? Why are you deliberately putting yourself through all of this?*

This went on for the full twenty minute ride. But there were no concrete answers to such introspection. Some people call it love. Others may even call it obsession. I don't suppose I tried to give it definition. I just knew I had to see her.

Chris had just gotten out of the shower when I got there. She was wearing a pair of bootie shorts and a towel wrapped around her chest. I took a seat in the sunroom while she went to throw something on.

I noticed all of her birthday cards arranged on the mantle above the fireplace and felt that sick feeling trying to take over my stomach. *You could've at least sent her a card*, I thought. But that was a flaw in my personality. I often found it very difficult to strike a nice median. I was an extremist. It was either all or nothing. And when I was done with something, I was done with it.

But apparently I wasn't yet done with Chris and everything that came along with her. Sitting there in the sunroom brought back fond memories. We often had breakfast in that room, shared a cup of coffee or simply sat around and talked. We had even stripped naked one day after a rigorous afternoon of bike riding and given up our bodies as the hot sun beamed in through the arched window and fell upon us.

Chris returned wearing a pair of very thin, loose silk pants with a matching top. It was navy blue with small, white polka dots, the soft material lightly falling on her sandaled feet. She sat at the table and made herself as comfortable as the awkward situation would allow.

"You're looking good," I said. "Looking real good."

"You, too, Kev."

We were gazing into each other's eyes the way we'd done so many times before. It seemed only natural for me to reach across the table and take her hands in my hands, slowly raise them to my lips and not once lose site of her stare. But such a gesture was rooted in emotion, and I couldn't allow emotion to take over reason.

It wasn't long thereafter that the tension eased up and we were once again engaged in one of our light, matter-of-fact conversations. Considering everything that had happened with us and the awkward interaction that remained between us, it actually turned out to be one of the best days we ever spent together.

There was a park nearby where Chris often went to read or just lounge under a big, shady tree. We decided to get out in the sun and spend a little time there. It was a gorgeous afternoon. The sky was clear and blue, the sun streaming down warm and bright. A gentle breeze seemed to whisper that spring had finally arrived.

Chris said that she had been to the park a few days earlier and had wanted to ride the swings, but as the park was filled with a bunch of screaming kids she was forced to forego child's play. But on that day there was only one kid, about three or four years old, tossing a ball around with his father. It was very peaceful in the park.

She and I removed our shoes and walked into the large sandy area that housed the swings.

"It reminds me of the beach," she said.

I looked down and saw that Chris was spelling her name in the sand with her toes. She was right. It did remind one of being at the beach. The sand was hot, yet strangely cold. It felt good between my toes as I joined Chris in her lazy play and also wrote my name.

"Will you push me, Kev?" she said, climbing into the swing and sticking her legs straight out.

I began pushing her back and forth, my hands sometimes resting on her lower back, sometimes on the roundness of her butt that protruded over the edge of the seat. Chris kept her legs extended straight in front of her as she sailed toward the sky, slowly drifted back and then bent her legs at the knees as she returned to my waiting hands. Back and forth, back and forth. Bend, straighten, bend, straighten.

"Not too high, Kev. I don't want to go too high," she said.

She reminded me of a kid, the way she found so much pleasure in such simple things, things that so many of us disregard in our calculated maneuvers through this hectic maze of a society. I loved and admired that about Chris. And I wanted a woman like that next to me, a woman who understood that there was more to life than simply making a lot of money, driving expensive cars and living in a big house. I wanted a woman who could remind me of the joys of life and not merely its empty distractions.

"Come swing with me," she said, lightly touching her feet to the ground and pushing herself.

I climbed into the swing next to her and began the slow, steady rocking back and forth motion until I had gained full momentum and was oscillating through the air like a suspended pendulum. I couldn't remember the last time I had enjoyed something so plain and simple. As Chris would swing back and pause high in the air for a brief moment before flying forward once more, I would twist my neck around and steal a quick look at her over my shoulder. She wore a look of contentment that seemed to come form deep within her sense of self. That was one of her special qualities. It never took much to make her happy.

Chris knew I didn't make a lot of money, but it didn't matter to her. I drove a raggedy-ass car and lived in a modest two-bedroom apartment that was only sparsely furnished. I didn't buy her extravagant gifts or take her to expensive places, but none of that mattered either. She said that she liked me for the person I was and that all she wanted was to simply be by my side. And that meant a lot to me.

Of course such an attitude invited comparison to so many I had seen in the past. I recall having tried to get with many Black women who, upon seeing the car I drove or learning the part of town in which I lived, never bothered returning my phone calls. It wasn't enough that I'm a pretty decent looking guy or that I have a college degree or that I'm a published writer or

that I cook a delicious shrimp vermicelli or that I keep
a clean place. It was what I didn't have that these
women sought in a man. And what I didn't have was a
front.

Granted, that's not to imply that White women
can't be just as superficial, nor does it imply that every
Black woman I've ever tried to talk to possessed such
a materialistic mentality. This obviously wasn't the case
with Jackie. But then again, like Chris, Jackie was a
very exceptional woman.

I had mentioned a movie review I read while we
were at Chris's place and suggested we leave the park
and go check it out. She and I stepped from the huge
sandbox onto soft, green grass. We took turns brushing
the sand from each other's feet and providing a supportive shoulder while we slipped on our shoes.
Walking back to the car, she and I seemed once again
drawn to each other by something beyond our control.
As if it were the only thing to do, without question and
without explanation, Chris's hand slipped into my
hand, and we slowly strolled through the park with the
look of springtime lovers.

Once Were Warriors, a drama about a New
Zealand family, was spell-binding and riveting. She and
I lingered in the parking lot for at least half an hour
replaying scenes that were either memorable or con-
fusing, interjecting comment or raising question. We
discussed it some more as we sat in a quaint Chinese
restaurant after the movie and had dinner. We both
agreed that it was the best film we'd seen in a very long
time. We also agreed that time spent apart had been
torture and that only in each other's absence did we

realize just how good things could sometimes be with us.

Although I never came right out and told Chris that the reason I broke off our relationship was because she was White, it was clearly understood. Chris knew quite well that race was a very real issue to me and that I held strong conviction about what was taking place in this country in regards to Black men. I never wanted to say it and I don't think Chris wanted to actually hear it, but now that everything was in the past there was a sense of distance that allowed her the necessary room to seek affirmation to what before was only suggestion. We were at her place later that evening drinking rum and coke.

"Kev," she said, "you never really did tell me why you broke things off."

I was softly jingling the ice around in my glass. It was dark in the room but I could slightly make-out her silhouette snuggled far back into the corner of the sofa as if in protective retreat.

"You only said that you could no longer do this," she continued. "What is it that you can't do?"

"Chris, you know how I feel about this."

"So it's my color. You can't be with me because I'm the wrong color."

I didn't say anything as a flush of embarrassment swept over me.

"Is that it, Kev? You don't want me because I'm White?"

"Yes," I said very softly. "That's it exactly. I can't be with you because you're White."

The words sounded dirty coming from my mouth.

It was like saying, "Sure, Chris, I'll fuck you but I don't want to be seen in public with you." I hated that Chris would make me come out and verbalize what we both already knew existed, and I hated it even more that I actually held such feelings. Although I was aware of what I felt inside, speaking the words aloud made the feelings real. They were offensive and insulting. Had she broken up with me for no other reason than the color of my skin, I would have been both hurt and upset. I probably would have labeled her a racist. But Chris seemed to take it all in stride. She seemed to understand exactly what I had been going through.

"I can imagine how you must feel," she said. "This is all new to you."

"Very new," I agreed.

"But it's a little different with me. I've dated several Black men before. In fact, I prefer Black men."

"You don't date White men, Chris?"

"Nope," she said quite matter-of-factly. "I hate White men. I hate their way of thinking, their smugness and conceit. I hate their entire culture."

Her claim was certainly a novelty. Usually such a rigid mindset of exclusively dating a specific group was reserved for one's own race. And I don't think there's anything very unusual about that. Compatibility is usually much easier to find within one's own racial clan as the result of viewing and approaching the world through a similar perspective. But to exclude one's own group suggested something far more reaching.

The first thing I thought about were those brothers who absolutely refuse to date Black women, who claim that Black women are too demanding, too hard to get along with, not oral enough, doesn't possess enough cultural or artistic interests, has too much of this, not enough of that. Whatever the reason, it always came down to the same end: Only a White woman could give them what they wanted and needed in a mate.

Such a blind, prejudicial attitude is a very scary thing. It is scary because the Black man who holds such a twisted view of his own women is just as mentally deformed and grotesque as the White woman who refuses to date Black men because they're supposedly all a bunch of wild, uneducated criminals who couldn't possibly have anything to offer her. Looking at it like that, I ventured even to regard Chris's attitude in the same manner. And of course I questioned my own attitude about whom I would or would not date. After all, wasn't I guilty of the same mentality by excluding White women from my pool of possible companions?

My dogmatic approach may have been applauded in the classroom but it wasn't that clean-cut when it came to real people in the real world. There remained that shady area of gray that left so much room for distortion. As I considered Chris's "preference" for Black men, Jackie's comment came back to me like an ominous warning. "That White woman was out to get you all along."

The first time Jackie said that I quickly brushed it off as her jealous insecurity talking. My arrogant nature even caused me to boast to myself, "Damn right she's out to get me. Chris knows a good thing when she sees it." But it wasn't until then that I actually considered the words. She was out to "get" me. Jackie's indirect warning, especially having learned of Chris's "preference" for Black men, was enough to cause definite concern. Yet concern wasn't a true deterrent. That quiet voice at the center of my soul was certainly whispering that something, somewhere wasn't quite right. It just wasn't right. But Reason spoke up much louder and said that I was simply being paranoid, that I was going too far with that "White America out to get the Black man" rhetoric.

Unfortunately, not listening to that voice held grave consequences. Several months later I would learn about another man, another Black man, Chris had been involved with in the past. And what I discovered, what I understood to have happened to this man who had given up so much to be with Chris, absolutely terrified me. Had I been able to foresee the potential danger that awaited me, I never would have gotten involved with her. But I wasn't afforded such insight as I was ultimately left to find out the hard way what the consequences were for getting involved with a woman like Chris.

"So, Chris," I said. "If you don't look at a person and see race, as is your claim, then why is it that you only date Black men? That seems very racial to me."

"It's not," she said.

"No?"

"Nope. Because it's not the race that attracts me. Although I admit I find darker skin tones more appealing."

"Then what is the attraction?"

"It's everything. The way Black men think and move and just their whole attitude. It's so much different than White men."

I was waiting for her to say the obvious, but Chris rarely said the obvious. She preferred to evade and suggest. So I gave her a little help.

"And what about the sex, Chris? Is the sex any different?"

"You mean between Black men and White men?"

"Yeah, Chris. Isn't that the attraction most White women have?"

"I don't know, Kev. I can't speak for most White women."

"Then speak for yourself."

"It all depends on the man," she said. "I've been with some White men who knew what they were doing in bed and I've been with some Black men who knew what they were doing as well. But I've also been with both Black and White who just didn't have a clue. It just all depends."

Chris unburied herself from in between the sofa cushions, slowly walked over to where I was sitting and stood over me. Standing there like that with her pale, alabaster skin and light eyes strikingly contrasted against a backdrop of darkness, she assumed the strange likeness of a vision or an image. She assumed the likeness of a ghost.

"I think I'll have another drink," she said. "You want one?"

"Yeah, sure. I'll have another one."

Chris fixed the drinks and then resumed her original spot on the sofa. Yet this time rather than drawing her legs to her chest in a defensive position, she extended them straight out and buried her feet beneath my legs.

"Is it okay if I put my feet here?" she asked. "They're getting a little cold."

"Yeah, sure."

I took a long swallow from my drink. It was good rum.

"Is it okay, Kev? Your drink? Is it strong enough?"

"Um-hum," I said, throwing my head back and making myself more comfortable.

Chris was slowly sipping her drink. I sat there in the dark and strained my eyes to see this woman who had become so intertwined in my life. But I couldn't see her. All I could make out was her outline, a vague and sketchy figure on the other end of the sofa. I knew there was a lot more to her than I was seeing, a lot more than she was willing to show me. But it would eventually come out; everything would come out. It was only a matter of time, something she and I had once again begun to share.

Sitting in the dark with Chris that night, I knew that things between us had gone into repeat. Neither of us ever said that we wanted to work on our differences and try to make things better. We simply did it.

I was nearly finished with my drink when shadows turned into form, shade became color. I initially thought that my eyes were beginning to adjust to the darkness, but I then noticed that the darkness had begun to lift and that a thin glow had infused the room.

"Look, " Chris said. "Isn't it beautiful?"

A full moon had slowly crawled across the sky and was peeping through the sunroom window. The light shining into the room was bright without being intense. It was actually quite soothing. And Chris was right; it was beautiful. She slid over next to me and snuggled real close, her head gently resting on my chest.

That's the magic I was telling you about," she whispered. "You remember?"

"Yeah," I said. "It's pretty."

We lay there holding each other and enjoying that wonderful spectacle in the sky. It was the simple things she loved most, and I too was beginning to love them.

"We had a very nice day," I said.

Chris pressed closer against me, slightly raised her head and gave me a soft kiss on the neck. Her lips were warm and moist.

"It's always good, Kev, always."

I've never been one to believe in fantasy. I consider myself a realist, and the fantastical has little place in the real world. But everything had been perfect that day. The late morning conversation in the sunroom, the afternoon at the park, the movie, dinner and now this beautiful evening. Lying there that night with Chris in my arms made me believe the unbelievable, For the first time in my life I knew, if only for a brief moment, that fairy tales sometimes do come true.

Chapter Thirteen

"What are you ?" I said.

Chris gave me a very puzzled look and scrunched up her face. That was one of her peculiarities. She scrunched up her face whenever something wasn't clear to her.

"What do you mean, what am I?"

"Are you a whore, Chris?"

She walked over to where I was standing and placed her hand on my crotch. She was gently stroking me up and down and staring intently into my eyes. I could feel the blood rushing down below, Chris's light caress bringing me to a swelling bulge.

"I'm your whore," she said with much seduction in her voice.

Great, I was thinking to myself. *Just what I've always wanted. My very own personal whore.* She started licking my bare chest and intermittently talking with her lips lightly pressed against my skin. Her breath was cool and tickling.

"All you have... to do... is tell me...how you.. want it," she said between licks. "I'll give it to you...any... way...you...like."

And she would. From behind, on her back, straddled on top of me, in the bed, in the kitchen, on the living room floor, the bathroom, sunroom, in front of my patio door with the blinds wide open. But none of this made Chris a whore. Actually, it had nothing to do with sex at all. It was simply her way of expressing affection for the man in her life and showing him that she was willing to follow his lead in whatever it was that made him happy. And in that she excelled. Chris definitely knew how to take care of her man.

She and I showered together often. Two, sometimes three times a day. Chris usually finished first. Upon doing so, she would dry herself and wait until I too had finished. Once I did get done, I would pull back the curtain and find her standing there with a thick, soft towel in her hand waiting for me to step out. Sometimes, especially in the morning, she would leave a glass of cold cranberry juice on the counter. Other times it was coffee, depending on my mood that day.

Breakfast was often served in bed. Chris would roll over and look at me with so much tenderness and love in her eyes that it almost hurt. With her head sunk deep down in the pillow, she would ask if I was hungry and, if so, what did I have a taste for.

"Would you like some pancakes?" she would first suggest.

I always smiled at this—smiled because Chris wasn't a very good cook, admittedly, but she did know how to fix a nice batch of pancakes. So it was usually that—pancakes, scrambled eggs, grilled cheese sandwiches, that sort of thing. It was never anything fancy but always seemingly with heartfelt emotion put into it all.

"Just roll over and get some more sleep," she would say, pulling the comforter up and tucking me in. "I'll be back in a little bit."

A little while later she would return with a round tray and place it in the center of the bed. She would then jump back under the covers with me as we sat there sharing breakfast, sat there sharing a very time-less moment. No matter how restless my sleep may have been the night before or how haunting the night-mares seemed, mornings like that always had a very calming effect on my erratic emotions. Chris's simplici-ty, her tenderness and devoted attention took me away from the daily strains of living. I didn't have to wear the mask, didn't have to play this role, watch my back, watch my front, step on this person, kiss this person's ass. I could simply be. For that, I wanted Chris close to me. For that, I loved Chris.

It was all so very different than previous relation-ships I'd had, relationships in which I was constantly catering to my woman's need while my own either went partially fulfilled or ignored altogether. Not even Jackie, whom I had tried from the very beginning to make happy, could appreciate what I did for her. The dinners and breakfasts I cooked, the baths I drew for her, lunches we had out, slow walks in the park, deep massages, pedicures, little surprise gifts left in her mail-box. All of this went without so much as a thank you. Not that I was expecting her to jump up and down and do tricks or anything like that. After all, I enjoyed doing these things for her. It made me feel good knowing I was making her feel god. But a simple "thank you" would have been nice, would have shown me that, if nothing else, she at least recognized and appreciated such attention.

As if her blind disregard weren't insulting enough, Jackie had even gone so far as to reduce the little things I did for her to a state of nothingness. We were talking one day several months after our break-up when she said with all earnest, "I don't even know why I wasted my time with you. You never did anything for me."

My grip tightened around the telephone as I felt myself either about to drop it on the floor in complete bewilderment or smash it against the wall in a fit of hot rage.

Had I heard her correctly?, I thought to myself. Surely she didn't say what I think she said. It must have been the six-pack I just drank that was whispering such nonsensical things in my ear.

"Jackie," I said, "what are you talking about I never did anything for you? I bent over backwards trying to make you happy. I was the one who was always having to keep the relationship intact, always trying to make what was wrong right."

"That's because you were the one always screwing things up."

I was absolutely floored that Jackie would hold such a thought. What exactly did she expect me to do–run out and buy her a house? I could hear my grandmother's voice so clearly it was as if we were all talking on a three–way line.

"See what I mean?" the voice said. "You try to treat a Black woman like she's the best thing in the world and she takes it all for granted. You can't be too nice to them, Kev. You have to stand up and put your foot down hard."

I later told my sister about the conversation Jackie and I had.

"Can you believe that?" I lamented. "Can you actually believe she said I never did anything for her?"

"Sure I can. Unless you consider sleeping behind her back doing anything for her."

Carmen didn't give it a second thought as she kept right along smacking on some wheat germ or soybean or some other bland, healthy shit she had recently gotten into.

"How can you say that?" I asked. "You know how hard I tried to make that thing work. You went with me that day to buy place mats and napkins and candles and all of that stuff when I fixed Jackie that really nice dinner."

She was wiping her mouth with one hand and waving me off with the other.

"See, Kev, what you don't understand is that not every woman is into that."

"Into what?"

"You know. Romantic dinners and bubble baths and massages. All of those things you were doing for Jackie."

"What are you talking about? Women eat that shit up."

"Don't get me wrong," she said. "I know some women like all of that. I suppose most women do. But not a woman like Jackie."

"And what's a woman like Jackie?"

"Well, first of all, she was already suspicious of you. Wasn't that what you told me?"

"Yeah."

Carmen popped a few bean sprouts in her mouth and crunched away.

"So if she's already suspicious, already assuming you're out to get something, then none of that comes across as genuine."

"But it was genuine. I really enjoyed treating her like she was special. Jackie was special."

"I know it was genuine," she said, "and to you it was genuine. But to her it just seemed like a big charade or a trick for something ulterior."

I sat there exasperated that something so simple, something so plain and simple, could have been turned into such a web of complexity. She continued with her armchair analysis.

"A woman like that, a woman who's been lied to and cheated on and misused by men in the past, isn't looking for any of that outward flash and obvious pretense. All she wants is a man who is going to be honest and caring, who is going to be a loyal husband to her and a good father to her children, a man who is going to go to work in the morning and come home in the evening. What she doesn't want is a man who has another woman over every time she goes out of town and forgets to call."

Damn, I thought. *A brother makes one mistake and it becomes his albatross.* Not only did Jackie hold this against me, but so, too, did my sister. I could detect a tinge of bitterness in her words. It seemed that she wasn't simply speaking on my ex-girlfriend's behalf, but also on her own behalf, as well as the behalf of every other woman who has ever been used, abused, and made confused by a man. And I think I'm safe in saying this is any woman who has ever known a man.

Although I'm her older brother, and I'm sure she accepts me without judgment, Carmen is still a woman and still a member of that group which shares a bond so deep and so special that it alludes most men. Her love may have been with me but her loyalty was with her gender. I got up to leave and was walking toward the door.

"Kev," she called out.

I turned back to see what she wanted. Carmen had this silly grin on her face that always took me back to our childhood. It reminded me of a photo we had taken together when she and I were five and six respectively. We looked very happy as we huddled close and gave the camera a big "cheese." This was before the long procession of funerals began and the nightmares wiped away all smiles.

"Yeah," I said. "What is it?"

"Would you like a tofu burger before you go?"

I gave my little sister a warm smile and shook my head.

"No," I replied. "I don't have much of an appetite."

Such reflection made it easy for me to understand why so many brothers went the other way, why they thought a White woman could give them something a Black woman was lacking. Because most of them could. A White woman, through a life of social indoctrination, plays a very passive and catering role to her man. It is what she's taught and what is expected of her. It thus becomes her nature. But this is hardly the case with Black women. She, like her male counterparts, is subjected to and must combat so much bullshit everyday of her life that in order to survive—not excel, but simply keep her emotional and mental sanity—she must adopt a more aggressive, active demeanor.

In so doing, a Black woman can't help but be stronger and less appeasing than a White woman. She doesn't have the time nor the emotional energy to waste on a man's insecurity and foolishness when she has to deal with so much of that already. In turn, a lot of men will construe a Black woman's strength as being hard, unfeminine and too difficult to deal with. And why should he have to settle for that when he could very easily have a woman who is willing, actually desiring, to put his needs before all else.

It was early May when I realized just how accommodating a White woman could be. My faithful '78 Celica, the car my grandmother bought me for my sixteenth birthday, finally called it quits. Well, not exactly. Actually, the car was still running strong (Japan was turning out their best cars back then), but it had an exhaust problem and was considered in violation of the noise pollution ordinance #153. As it cost more to quiet the exhaust than the car was worth, I simply said a few kind words over it and finally gave it its due rest.

Not living on a bus line and having always had a car, I was initially quite intimidated by the idea of not having such convenience and freedom that a car affords, especially living in such a widely spread out city as Atlanta. But Chris was right there to pick up the slack. If I needed to go to the grocery store, Chris saw to it that I got there. If I needed a ride to work, Chris picked me up. If I needed to take care of business while she was at work, Chris gladly left me her car. If I needed to wash clothes, Chris swooped them up from my place and took them home with her. And she did this all without hesitation.

"Thanks a lot," I would say. "I really do appreciate this."

"You know you're welcome, Kev," she would reply with much joy and contentment beaming from her eyes.

It was very easy to love Chris when she so freely extended herself and showed such caring and devotion. It also made it easier to deal with that inner struggle I had felt in the past whenever we went out. Of course, we still received the stares, but it no longer mattered. I knew Chris was the best thing to come into my life and that in my life was where I wanted her to remain. As far as everyone else I simply thought, *That's right, this White woman is my lady. And she's a very fine lady. She doesn't care that I used to drive a raggedy car and now I drive no car. She doesn't care that my bank account may be in a little slump. This woman loves me for who I am and what I'm about. She looks out for me and makes sure I have what I need. She isn't all wrapped up in what I can do for her, where I can take her or what I can buy her. She makes sure my needs are met, makes sure I feel good both physically and emotionally. And if you don't like it, then fuck you. Plain and simple. Fuck youuu!"* To add exclamation to it all, I would pull Chris even closer to my side and give her a big, sloppy kiss.

The sisters couldn't stand it and I didn't give a damn. None of them had ever given me the things Chris gave. Yet, unknowingly, none of them took so many of the things Chris was taking. Although she attended to my needs willingly, she didn't attend to them without charge. It seems that Chris was keeping tabulation of expenditures from day one. It was only a matter of time before she came to collect the debt.

Chapter Fourteen

There is good and there is bad in us all. That my car had become indisposed was occasion enough for Chris to show me how good she could be. It also did just the opposite.

As I knew I would have to buy a new car, and buy one soon, I had taken on a second job working in the library to supplement my income as a substitute teacher. By the middle of May, I had saved up enough money for a down payment and was ready to embark on something I had never done in my life. I was ready to buy my first brand new car.

At the same time, Chris too was preparing to make a little expedition of her own. As she had been feeling stressed out lately, she decided to take a few days off work and drive down to the beach. The night before I was to go car shopping and Chris was to depart for a little R&R, she stayed over at my place. With her bags packed and ready to go, she had planned to leave the next morning and drive directly to Daytona.

The night before she left was a good night. We had sex so intense that it seemed as if it were either the first or the last time we had gotten together. We then strolled naked to the kitchen, fixed a snack to eat and drank a couple of beers. Time thereafter was spent in conversation. Not only had the night gone well, but it seemed that our relationship had taken on a new, fuller dimension altogether.

Chris and I were having serious discussion about her enrolling in the writing workshop. Fully aware of the problems it may cause with Jackie also being in the program, Chris and I both agreed that if there were in fact a problem, it was Jackie's own problem and not ours. We often talked about getting a place together. Even conversation of marriage and children would pop up from time to time.

Chris said that she would marry me without hesitation had I asked her. But of course this was all idle talk. Although I knew I wanted a wife and family one day, I wasn't ready to make such a commitment right at that moment. And I definitely wasn't ready to father a child, though Chris would often stand next to me as we stared into the bathroom mirror and comment how beautiful our children would be. Yet there would be no children, there would be no marriage, there would be no place of our own. Something was about to happen that would alter the course of our relationship and the course of our lives forever.

The next morning was bright and sunny. It was supposed to be the start of something really good. I was about to buy a new car and Chris was only a few hours away from a much needed getaway. We stood at her car and said our good-byes.

"Kev," she said, "are you going to miss me much?"

"I'm already missing you, girl. Already missing you."

Hug, hug, kiss, kiss.

"You drive safely, Chris."

"Okay, Kev. I'll give you a call when I get there."

"Yeah, you do that," I said, a blurred vision of Jackie invading my mind and trespassing against this very tender moment spent with my lady. Get away! Get away!

"And good luck with your car," she yelled over her roughly idling engine that was in desperate need of a tune-up.

"Thanks!," I yelled back.

I stood in the parking lot and watched as Chris slowly drove away. I had not lied either. I was already missing her, already looking forward to her return. Unfortunately, the Chris I had grown to love and care so much about would never make it back from the beach. It was instead a total stranger who would return in Chris's place, her only souvenirs a bag filled with emotional havoc and grief.

Chapter Fifteen

"What?" I said. "You must be kidding."

The White salesman sat calm and poised on the other side of the desk. He placed his fingers to his temple, his elbow resting on a large stack of papers and files. His head was cocked to the side in a very condescending manner I'd seen over and over and over, the look of which seemingly asking what right did I have for taking up so much of his valuable time.

"That's the best I can do," he said. "The best, that is, considering your credit history."

"What's wrong with my credit?"

"Well," he began, folding his hands together in front of him on the desk. He was being very serious. "It seems, Mr. Luttery, that you have quite a bit of unpaid student loans."

Those fucking student loans, I thought. *I wish those pricks would get off my back. I said they would get their money. They know they'll get their money, one way or another.*

"But as I said," the man continued, "we do have a program that would allow you to reestablish your credit."

What was he talking about, reestablish my credit. There was nothing wrong with my credit. Sure, I may have had a late payment here, a late payment there, and of course the student loans I still owed, but there were people who had far worse credit than I and were driving around in new cars, buying houses and doing whatever else they wanted to do.

"As far as the terms, Mr. Luttery, that's the best I can do."

"Three thousand down and four-ten a month?" I asked.

Knowing that I probably wasn't about to buy, he didn't waste any more words but simply gave me a short nod. I left the Honda dealer both shocked and angry. Mostly I was angry. There I was working two jobs with twelve hundred to put down and he was taking me through all of these changes over a Civic, a god-damn, entry-level, twelve thousand dollar Civic. I marveled at the way he sat there demanding a three thousand dollar down payment and a note as high as four hundred and ten dollars, all of this without so much as a smile, though I know inside he was probably cracking the hell up.

I got back home that afternoon and was still pissed off. What did that salesman think I was, a fool, a child, a (yes, I dare to say it) woman? No, it's quite obvious what I am. I'm a Black man, a Black man who had the down payment, had the income, had the credit, had everything I was supposed to have. Still I was being jerked around.

I poured myself an ice-cold beer and fell on the bed while I checked my messages. The only person who had called that I was glad to hear from was Chris.

Her message said: "Hi, Kev, it's me. I was just calling to let you know I got in okay. The drive up was really long. It's so hot out and you know my air doesn't blow all that cold. Well, anyway, I'm about to take a shower and maybe lay out on the beach for a while. Hope you're doing okay and the car shopping is going well. Missing you and loving you. Bye."

The recorded voice came on and asked to "push seven to erase this message, push nine to save." I pushed nine. The voice said: "Message will be saved for three days."

I took a long swallow of beer and rolled over on my back. I lay there watching the ceiling fan spin round and round, my mind trying hard not to think about the incident at the Honda dealer. I instead thought about Chris and the message she had left.

"Yeah," I softly said aloud, " I'm missing you too, girl." Missing her so much that I played and replayed that message every day that she was gone.

I was up and out early the next morning. My uncle was kind enough to let me borrow his car to do my running around and I didn't want to be gone all day in it. As I knew Toyotas were very good cars, I decided to check those out.

I walked onto the lot and knew immediately that I had to have the black Celica that was sitting there. I had read about their performance, value, reliability, blah, blah, blah, blah, and was itching to take it out on the road and stomp my foot into it. But stepping on the Toyota lot was like stepping into a three ring circus. I thought the scene the day before was a farce, but this, well...

Step right up! Step right up! Popcorn, peanuts! Step right up! Get your cotton candy today! Step right up! Step right up!

"Five thousand," the ring leader said.

I sat on the edge of my seat in total awe. My God, he was incredible. What more could he do to possibly top that. Anticipation mounted as he began performing his magic, and then reaching into his bag of tricks he pulled out a big, fat, whopping...

"Three-ninety a month."

I tried to control my stutter but there was no way.

"You you you mean I have to ppput down five thousand?"

"That's right."

"And and and my note wwwould still be three-ninety?"

"That's right."

I slumped back in my seat not knowing what else to say. This was one of the few times in my life that I was actually at a lost for words. In just a flash, I replayed the way in which I had lived my life up to that point and tried to find the small crack through which I must have slipped. Let me see, I thought. I graduated from high school and went to college. I studied very hard, earned a 3.5 and then received my B.A. I came home and taught high school English for a year. I hadn't gotten locked up, didn't have unsupported kids sprinkled all over the place, wasn't strung out on the pipe. I went to work every day and did a little freelance writing on the side. I diligently saved my money, got my paperwork in order and now was ready to buy a car. Not a fat Lexus or a Benz or even the top of the line Supra. Just a nice, sporty little fifteen thousand dollar mid-level Toyota.

Thinking I must have heard him incorrectly, I inquired once more.

"Five thousand down and three-ninety a month?"

"That's right."

Damn, five thousand down. I wasn't trying to buy a house. It was only a car, a fifteen thousand dollar car. It was unheard of. It was ridiculous. It was thirty-three percent! I didn't have that, and I didn't foresee having it for a very long time. The ring leader must have seen the disappointment and frustration on my face.

"I know it sounds like a lot," he said.

NO FUCKING KIDDING!!

"But that's the only way any of the lending institutions will carry your loan."

"I'm sorry," I said. "I just don't understand. As much money as I make and the down payment I'm...."

"Oh, don't get me wrong," he defended. "You make really good money. No one's disputing that. And your credit is fine."

I was wondering how my credit could be fine with this dealer but not with the other.

"But the problem, Mr. Luttery, is that you've never financed a new car before. And that concerns all of the banks we go through. They simply won't carry a fifteen thousand dollar loan unless you put down five thousand."

"And the note would still be almost four hundred?" I asked.

He was slowly nodding his head up and down. Had I been a little more on the edge, just a little closer to that breaking point, I probably would have reached across the desk, grabbed him by that ugly polyester tie he was wearing and choked him to death. But as I didn't go there to murder anybody, just to purchase a car, I got up and politely excused myself from the office.

I was halfway across the showroom floor when the ringleader ran up from behind and stopped me.

"Now," he said, "of course we have some nice used models, '90's, '91's, that I'm sure we could put you in."

I fought back the urge to go off and simply said, with the teenie weenie bit of politeness still left in me, "No. A used car just won't do right now."

"Still under warranty," he added.

"No, I think what I'll do is go talk to my credit union and see what they say. I may be back."

I had been to two places, both times dealing with Whites, both times having the door slammed shut in my face. I didn't know why I thought going to my job's credit union would be any different. In fact, I didn't think it would be any different. I was still dealing with Whites and thus still dealing with the same shit.

"No, Mr. Luttery," the redhead man at the credit union said. "I'm sorry but we are unable to extend you the loan at this time."

Feeling a sense of suffocation closing in around

me, I desperately pushed against the imaginary walls and tried to keep them off. I thought that if they couldn't approve me for fifteen thousand then maybe I could get the five thousand I needed to make that outrageous down payment.

"I'm sorry," the Dennis the Menace look-alike said again, "but you just don't qualify at this time."

I withdrew all of my money from the credit union, closed my account and told that White man to kiss my ass. With nothing left to lose, I took my down payment and went to the bank. There is a Wachovia not far from where I grew up and was now run by Black women. Every now and then there was an occasional White woman working there, maybe a White man, seldom a brother but always, always swarming with Black women.

"Let me go talk to one of these sisters," I said to myself the same day Dennis the Menace gave me two consecutive no's.

The bank manager's name was Gwendolyn Sparks. I'll never forget that woman. She was medium brown with very full features. Her lips were full, her hips and thighs were full, even her calves were full and developed. But she was hardly fat. She was what I would call "thick." She stood almost six feet, and was clearly that height with heels. Her hair was tinted a sort of auburn brown, maybe hazelnut or something, and cut short. It looked good on her and further accentuated her high, prominent cheekbones and dark brown eyes. When she walked across the office, her steps were punctuated with a sound of distinct authority. The skirt she was wearing wasn't tight, at least not unprofessionally tight, but it hugged her body just enough to show what she was carrying back there. And like most Black women, she was toting a nice little package.

During my first meeting with Mrs. Sparks I couldn't help but notice the difference between her and Chris. Although Chris was a very attractive, sexy woman, she didn't have that rich womaness that Mrs. Sparks possessed. In fact, had the two been in the same room, Chris would've seemed like a little girl next to this very womanly woman. I had seen some of this in Jackie, as such a quality tends to be endemic to most Black women, but not even she could match the aura of provocative strength that seemed to emanate from Mrs.Sparks.

The strange thing about my initial encounter with Mrs. Sparks is that, despite my having always been around Black women, she seemed almost exotic, like something I've long yearned yet never tasted. I found Chris very arousing, and I loved Chris, but she just didn't have that, that, that "umph!" most Black women have. She couldn't have it, as this is an attitude fostered out of a unique set of experience that in no way would Chris ever share as a White woman.

That was the first time since crossing to the other side that I realized I was beginning to miss Black women. The longing nostalgia would later grow to an intensity that seemed almost mocking. Chris and I would go out sometimes and I had to literally fight with myself to keep from staring at other women. It didn't matter where we went.

Once we attended an arts festival in the park and I damn near had a fit. It was a beautiful summer day and the park was filled with some of the finest Black women in Atlanta. I tried to be considerate as Chris and I strolled hand-in-hand checking out the various exhibits. But I swear, it seems like we couldn't walk ten yards without passing a woman so fine I probably would have paid her to go out with me. Like I said, I tried to be considerate. I didn't want to disrespect my lady by drooling all over these other women. But it was impossible to deny the obvious when it was staring me right in the face.

I would cast discreet (and sometimes not so discreet) glances at one of the many women flaunting a knock-out body, look at the woman on my arm and then once again fix my eyes on that body. I would slowly shake my head and say to myself, "Damn, Kev, look at what your ass is missing out on."

It wasn't only the bodies and attractive faces either. It was the whole persona I was missing. I was at a nail shop getting a manicure one afternoon when I began to make true sense of what I had been feeling. There were several women sitting around talking, and I was watching them all as Yvette filed and buffed my nails to a high shine. What I couldn't help noticing was the way in which they interacted with one another, their mannerisms and gestures, the way in which they held their heads, moved their arms and the furtive glances that were exchanged back and forth. I was listening to the musical pitch and tone in their voices that seemed almost ageless, seemed to speak more to the heart and soul than to the audible ear. The room was filled with deep, robust laughter, wide, sparkling grins and talking hands, all so familiar, all so comforting.

Though it was such a simple thing, such a natural part of being Black that I had lived everyday of my life, I suddenly felt that I was no longer included in this ritualistic gathering. It was as if I were a stranger, an outsider who had crawled under the fence of self-exile and eavesdropped on what before had been shared with open invitation. I felt like a perverted voyeur who had trespassed against something very private and intimate. For I had crossed to the other side, unbeknownst to them, and yet still had the audacity to sit there and relish in their company. There was no doubt about it. I was really missing my Black women that day.

"Mr. Luttery?" she said.

"Yes."

"I'm Gwendolyn Sparks. Would you like to step into my office."

She led me into a very comfortable office, walked around behind the desk and motioned for me to take a seat. She too sat, clasped her hands together in front of her and leaned slightly forward.

"Now, what can I do for you today?" she asked.

I could detect that ring of genuine interest in her voice. There was no condescension, no apathy, no bullshit.

"I need to buy a car."

I was very simple and to the point. I went on to explain how much I had to put down, showed her my pay stubs, utility bills, all of the other necessary paperwork. In turn Mrs. Sparks crunched some figures on her computer and read off various interest rates depending on my down payment and whether I opted to carry the loan for forty-eight months or sixty months.

Everything in her voice and attitude was positive and upbeat. She spoke as if I had already been approved.

"Let me put your information in the computer," she said, "and pull your credit file."

"Okay."

"Give me a call back at, oh, say about three-thirty. I should know something by then."

"Thank you very much," I said as I extended my hand.

She gave me a gentle handshake and said I was welcome.

It seemed as if 3:30 would never get here. I lingered around my apartment and tried to keep my body busy and my mind preoccupied. But of course all I kept thing about was the loan and how far up shit's creek I would be if she too came back with a negative verdict. My only recourse would be to spend the next few months busting my ass even more than I'd already been doing and trying to save up enough money to play the game that had been introduced.

After much anxiety and mental torture, Judgment Time had finally arrived. I dialed the number very slowly and tried as best I could to maintain my composure. *Stop shaking,* I told myself. *It's just a car loan. So what if she says no. You've heard that four times already. No big deal. It's not the end of the world. It's just money.*

"Hello, Wachovia Greenbriar. How may I direct your call?"

"Gwendolyn Sparks, please."

"May I ask who's calling?" the anonymous voice quizzed.

"Yes, it's Kevin Luttery."

"Just one moment, please."

There was a deafening silence on the other end of the line. No easy–listening music or promotional advertisement or anything like that. Just silence and anticipation. I realized that I was unconsciously swallowing over and over, although my mouth was dry and fuzzy, almost as it is the morning after a long night of fierce drinking. And then:

"Hello, Kevin?" a voice finally said.

"Yes, I'm here."

"Listen, I was just going over your paperwork now and..."

Her voice trailed off and died. There was that distinct pause that is so often the attendant of bad news. Terror seized my senses.

"Yes," I said with a dull, sickening lump in my throat.

"And as everything seems fine and in order, I would be more than happy to give you the loan."

My body went slightly limp as I released the air I had been holding in my lungs. My mouth moistened and the tight lump in my throat relaxed. For the past five minutes I had been standing before my bedroom window unable to move, those suffocating walls closing in more and more. I now stepped away from the window and walked, damn near skipped, out of my bedroom and down the hallway. I don't know if I've ever said the words "thank you" as much or in so many different ways as I did at that moment.

"It's my pleasure, " Mrs. Sparks said. And that was that.

Within two days I had closed on the loan and was driving off the lot in my first new car. It felt good. Not simply owning a new car, but it felt good that the whole nasty ordeal had come to an end. I'm sure buying a new car is supposed to be an exciting, fun experience, but the fun and excitement had eluded me as I came eye to eye with the most obvious discrimination I've ever felt.

The immense stress had broken out my skin, stolen my sleep and suppressed my appetite. The differential treatment I received had forced me, if only for a second to validate my position in a society that does not welcome me.

That was all behind me now. I had trodden through a den of quiet hatred and walked away the victor. I attained what I had gone in search of and did it all without having to compromise my dignity or sense of self-worth. I had gotten my car. Everything was going to be okay now. It was the end of the week and Chris, the woman I loved, would once again be in my arms and in my life. At least that is how it all appeared.

Chapter Sixteen

She appeared perfectly herself, whoever that self may have actually been. There was the same laid-back tone and pace to her voice, the same false starts and hesitations as she deliberated over her words like a judge in chambers. Once assured that she would not offend or incite, she easily slipped back into the calm facade that had become her second skin. The strained, almost forced, laughter was still there, and I assume it will always be there. For it is this that makes the deceptive image seem so very real. Like a magician's subtle slip of the hand, her affected laughter had a way of diverting attention whenever outward appearance threatened to break down and expose her true self. Now you see me, now you don't.

Chris spent a few minutes sharing the small details of her trip and then, with a touch of excitement in her voice, said, "Soooo?" probably bobbing her head from side to side.

"So what?" I replied.

"You know what. Did you get your car?"

"Yeah, I got it."

"You did?" She let her excitement escape her. "What did you get?"

"I got another Celica."

"Kev, that's wonderful. You must be excited."

"Yeah, I suppose so."

"I remember how excited I was when I bought my first new car," she said. "I didn't have any money to put down and had just started a new job making little or nothing. All I had was a piece-of-shit Prelude that was probably only worth about three or four hundred dollars. But I drove off in a new car that very same day."

"That's very interesting," I commented, more to myself than to Chris. And it was interesting.

"So when are you going to drive up and let me see it?"

"I don't know, Chris. Some time soon I suppose."

I didn't mean to be short with her or to sound rude, but I'm sure that's how it appeared nonetheless. There was a moment of strained silence. Chris must have sensed that there was a problem because she didn't say anything. Even twenty miles away and over the phone could I feel her uneasiness. I'm sure she was thinking the problem would go away if she didn't acknowledge it. That was her solution to so much around her. If she looked the other way so as not to see the problem, then the problem was not real. That which is not acknowledged simply is not so. But as I wasn't saying anything and the silence between us grew louder, she had little choice but to acknowledge it.

"What's wrong, Kev?" she asked without wanting to ask.

I began slowly and deliberately. I wanted to share with her what I had gone through during the past few days, but at the same time I wanted to be certain I did not unfairly vent my anger in her direction.

"These past few days..." I started.

"Yeah, Kev? Did something happen?"

There was a concern in her usually calm voice which caused it to slightly sway, caused it to waver as if tiptoeing right up against the edge of fear.

"Chris, buying this car was one of the most stressful ordeals of my life. It was worse than grueling college finals or any job interview I've ever had."

"Yeah," she agreed. "It does stress you out."

How the fuck would she know about being stressed out?, I thought. *Her prissy little white ass just waltzed onto the lot with no money, little income, no job stability, and drove away in a new car just like that. How the fuck....*

Stop Kev. This is exactly what you said you didn't want to do. It's not her fault. She has nothing to do with this. I took a deep breath, let my mind clear for a moment and then continued.

"My skin broke out," I said, adding, "and I haven't hardly eaten or slept in three days."

"Was it that bad?"

"The first place I went was a Honda dealer. I had all of my paperwork in order. Had my money and everything."

"And what happened?"

"I'll tell you what happened. The White motherfucker on the other side of the desk gave me some bullshit about my credit being messed up. My student loans. Said I would have to put down three thousand on a little Civic and the note would still be over four hundred. Can you believe that shit? Three thousand down and four-ten a month for a Civic."

"I guess it does sound a bit steep," Chris admitted, her voice mild, almost meek, and far away. She had assumed the appeasing tone one might have if locked in a room with a known psychopath and seeing his evil half waking up right before one's very eyes.

"If you think that's crazy," I said, "listen to this. The next day I went to check out some Toyotas and had the same smelly shit tossed in my face. But this time it wasn't my credit standing in the way. The punk-assed salesman claimed he couldn't find a bank that would carry the loan for fifteen thousand. Said since I've never financed a car before that I was a high risk or some shit like that."

"Oh," she added, her tone greatly diminished next to my hot ranting.

"But he was willing to sell me a car alright. For five thousand down and three-ninety a month. Can you believe that? Five fucking thousand down."

I sat there reliving it all in my head, my mental screen capturing a picture of the ring leader as he sat smug and arrogant in his little cubbyhole office. I remember stepping in and glancing around the office with what must have been a look of distaste. The salesman caught my eye and exchanged a look of his own which seemed to say "I know it ain't much, but it's more than enough for your black ass. Now sit down and let's get this thing over with."

Chris's very paced and calculated voice slowly brought me back to the present.

"So, Kev, what happened? You said you got the car. Something must have gone your way."

"Let me tell you. I left the Toyota place and went to the credit union. I was going to see if maybe they would be a little more helpful, considering they had been holding onto my money all this damn time. So I go there, right, and once again I have to deal with this White man who, in a way, holds a small piece of my fate right there in his grubby little fingers. So I fill out the application and everything and, not to my surprise, the prick says no, says he's sorry but they're unable to approve me at this time. So here's what I do, okay? Chris, you listening?"

"Yes," she said.

"So what I do is turn right back around and apply for five thousand to use for that big, ridiculous down payment. As crazy as I knew it was, I was actually going to do it. But of course he turned me down for that as well. Two no's, Chris. Two loud, resounding NO's!!"

I could sense that passion rising in me and about to explode. But I didn't want to explode in front of Chris. She was much too sensitive and probably would've become frightened had I shown her all of the anger I was still feeling. I walked into the kitchen and got a beer, hoping the hops and barley would keep the anger at a safe distance. Don't explode, I kept reminding myself. Don't explode.

"So here's what happened," I said. "I ended up going to Wachovia and getting the loan. I said, 'Let me go talk to one of these sisters at the bank and see if they can hook me up.' And sure enough, I got my money just like that."

I could feel the anger subsiding, the beer rushing to my head and quieting my boisterous temper.

"That's good," Chris said.

"I don't know why I didn't go there in the first place, instead of wasting my time with those White motherfuckers and getting all stressed out and everything."

"I'm sorry it wasn't a good experience for you," she said. "But I really wish you wouldn't do that."

"Do what?"

"You know. Keep pointing out that they were White."

"Well, they were White."

"Yeah, so what? That has nothing to do with anything."

I was about to take a swig from my beer but stopped just as the bottle reached my lips. I slowly brought it down and set it on the windowsill.

"What?" I asked, very calmly though quite deliberately.

"You keep talking about them being White like it matters one way or the other."

"And it doesn't?"

"Of course not,"she said.

"You know, Chris, you're absolutely right. It's not so much their being White as it is my being Black."

"Kev, don't."

"Don't what?"

"Don't try to turn this into a racial thing."

"That's what it is, Chris. The whole ordeal was a racial thing."

"See," she said. "That's your biggest problem. You think every White person is a racist, that every White person has some vendetta against you just because you're Black and is somehow out to get you. No matter what it is, Kev, you always find a way to attach race to everything. I really wish you would lighten up with all of that."

"Lighten up? Is that what you're saying I should do? I should lighten up on something that affects me and my world in so many different ways? Huh, Chris? Is that what you're saying?"

"All I'm saying is that I don't believe a car salesman would intentionally not sell you a car just because you're Black. He works on commission. Turning your business away would be doing more harm to himself. I just can't believe it. If you have the money and a good job and pretty decent credit, then it just doesn't make sense that he wouldn't sell you a car just because you're Black. I don't believe it."

I felt the passion begin to stir once again and the anger woooossh up in my head like a violent whirlwind. As it began to twist and turn in a blind fury, I could hear that little voice at the pit of my soul—quiet, very, very quiet—whispering to me with all rationale, "wake up, wake up, wherever you are."

"Then you tell me," I said. "If it wasn't about race then what was it?"

"My God, Kev, I don't know. It probably was your credit or what the man said about never financing a car before."

"I'm telling you it wasn't my credit. And as far as never financing a car before, well, you just said yourself that you bought your first new car with nothing. No down payment, no real income, no job stability. Nothing but a raggedy trade-in."

"You can't look at every situation in the same light, Kev."

"Or maybe you had more to offer than a trade-in," I suggested.

"What is that supposed to mean?"

"I don't know. May be you gave the salesman some of that delicious head you're so good for."

As soon as the words escaped my mouth I realized how nasty and rude it all sounded. I told myself that I wasn't going to turn my anger around and throw it on her, that I wasn't going to hurt Chris because of something beyond her control. But this wasn't the Chris I had known. I wasn't sure who this person was who stood a mere breath away from calling me an outright liar.

"Kev," she said. "I told you I'm not like that. I only share that with the man I'm with and the man I love. I think you owe me an apology."

"Yeah, yeah, yeah. I've heard all of that old shit before. It's this new shit I'm interested in."

"What shit?"

"Your shit."

"What are you talking about, my shit? My shit what?"

"I'm talking about your insinuation that none of this happened. That it's all simply in my head, make-believe, a mere figment of my paranoid mind."

"I never said it was in your mind," she defended. "I just don't understand it."

"I don't expect for you to understand it. You can't understand it because you aren't in my skin when I cross the street and hear all of those car locks click, click, clicking, or when I pass a White couple on the street and the guy pulls his woman close to his side like I automatically want her skinny ass just because she's White, or when I flip on the news and hear how Republicans have descended onto Congress with bill-slashing scythes sharp and in hand. No, I don't expect you to understand any of that."

"Then why are we even having this conversation?"

"Because I expect for you to want to understand. And if nothing else, I at least expect for you to keep all of that 'it's just in your head' bullshit to yourself."

"Kev..."

"It's not in my damn head," I interrupted. "Here I am making good money with twelve–hundred cash to put on the table and these White pricks are telling me I don't qualify for a fifteen thousand dollar loan. And then I go to the bank and talk to one of my own, and I get the money just like that. You tell me that's all in my head."

"It may not be in your head," she agreed. "It may simply be that the lady at the bank bent a few rules in your favor. Instead of pointing an accusatory finger at White America, maybe you should just be thankful there's someone in the system looking out for you."

"Some way of showing my thanks," I said aloud to myself.

"What was that?"

I didn't bother to answer as my thoughts were fixed on what Chris had just said. She was absolutely right; I should have been thankful. I had gone to three different institutions and they had all slammed the door in my face. The only person who was willing to extend a helping hand was Gwendolyn Sparks, a Black woman. And how was I about to show my thanks? I was about to take advantage of her favor so that I could drive just a little faster, just a little more reliably, just with a little more style to see my White girlfriend.

Not just any White girlfriend, but my White girlfriend who could not understand, who didn't care to understand, what I was talking about. My White girlfriend who couldn't be bothered with it all, who wanted to look the other way and pretend that it never happened. My White girlfriend who wanted me, having just lived it first-hand, to believe that it never happened. My White girlfriend who, while I was down here dealing with a bunch of shit, was off lying on the beach. My White girlfriend who, all jazz-loving, Black-fucking aside, was still a member of that institution that had spat in my face and shut the door over and over again.

It was the first time in quite a while that I was feeling that numbing sense of betrayal. I thought about what Chris said, about the lady at the bank bending a few rules in my favor, and wondered would she have been so accommodating had she known of my situation. Probably not, I concluded.

I could hear Mrs. Sparks as she sat at her desk feeding my application through the paper shredder. "If he's stupid enough to be with a woman like that, then he probably shouldn't be on the street operating a vehicle anyway."

I'm not sure how long, but it must have been a very long time before I said anything else. Chris's words just sort of faded in as I realized I had been standing there holding the phone, my mind trying very hard to bring structure to an arrangement of disjointed thoughts and emotions.

"...wrong?" she said.

"What?"

"I said what's wrong" Chris repeated. "I've been talking to you but you aren't listening."

What was wrong, I thought. The words didn't even sound real, like the unreal faces staring at me in the restaurant that morning over breakfast, the hollow mouths and empty words all unreal. I didn't know whether it was more appropriate to laugh or to cry. What was wrong, the lady wants to know.

"Kev, I don't mean to sound insensitive."

"Of course not," I muttered.

"Because I know how strongly you feel about all of this. It's just that I know there's more to you than that. You don't need to do that, Kev. Really, you don't."

"I don't need to do what?"

"You know, blame everything on race."

"Is that what you think I do?" I said, my voice very, very calm.

"That's what you're doing now. And that's what a lot of people do."

"You mean a lot of Black people?"

"Well, yeah. Especially Black men."

If it weren't for the car shopping ordeal having stolen my appetite and thus leaving me with nothing in my stomach but air and a little bit of beer, I would have thrown up all over the floor. I could feel the muscles twisting and contracting in tight knots, my mouth suddenly filled with saliva the way it does just before a fit of vomiting. But there was nothing to vomit, only the nauseating sensation and an occasional spasm of dry retching in my throat. Who was this strange person on the other end of the phone voicing such strange opinion? And what had happened to my Chris? Where was the woman I fell in love with and thought was the best thing to have come into my life? Had she washed out to sea while lying on the beach trying to add some color to her skin? Was she washed out into the silent depths below where no one could see who she really was because there are no eyes and there is no light, only a perpetual darkness behind which to hide?

"You know it's true," she said. "You have to admit it yourself. A lot of Black men use that race bullshit as a crutch whenever they fall below the margin. If they don't get the job or get the raise or get the loan or get the test score or this or that, the first thing they do is point a finger and cry racism. I'm sure you know what I'm talking about whether you want to admit it or not."

Yes, I did know what she was talking about. There are men, and women, who place far too much emphasis on how others are holding them back instead of looking at the various ways in which they may be holding their own selves back. But I also know that racism is very much alive and thriving, and that it wasn't simply a weak cop-out. I know that I personally was taking care of business rather than sitting around crying about the White man did this to me and the White man

did that to me. And that was the difference. I had gotten my education, I was making good money, I had
published in two widely-circulated, widely-respected
magazines. And things for me were just getting started.

Still, I wasn't one of these blind fools running
around thinking that because I had a little of this and a
little of that, I was somehow set apart and exempt from
the masses of those with whom I share more than outward skin tone, but to whom I am indefinitely bound
by history and by circumstance form cradle to grave. I
didn't appreciate anyone accusing me of copping out,
and I sure as hell didn't appreciate the accusation coming from my White girlfriend.

"But you don't have to do that," Chris continued.
"You're very smart and educated and ambitious. I see
that, Kev. I see you going after whatever you want and
getting it. That's why I don't understand it when you
start wasting so much of your time and energy talking
and complaining instead of just doing."

I sat on the edge of the bed and rested my throb-
bing forehead in the center of my hand. I wished to
God she would just shut the fuck up, that the dull dron-
ing on and on of that foreign voice would cease and,
as if awaking from one of those horrible nightmares, I
would once again hear Chris's own calm, even voice
whispering sweet suggestions in my ear. That strange,
strange voice droned on.

"Kev, I know some of the things I say may not be
what you want to hear. And I know we don't see things
eye to eye all the time. But I've told you before how I
am, and I mean it. It's just that I'm not so sure you
believe me. But I want you to believe me, Kev. I want

you to know I'm telling the truth when I say that..."

"I know,Chris. I know. You aren't like most White people."

It was more than either of us could have expected. The words seemed to take a step beyond mere sarcasm. It was as if they served as the closing remarks to the whole farcical event I had experienced over the past few days. As clever as she was at stepping in and out of her skin, Chris could very easily have been a sideshow act herself, a slight diversion in what had been an elaborate, ridiculous hoax. Step right up! Step right up! See for yourselves the Lady With the Changing Faces!

"Are you okay, Kev?" she asked.

"Yeah," I lied. "I'm fine."

"Listen, I hope what happened with the car dealer, whatever that may have been about, isn't going to affect things with me and you."

She hesitated for my reassurance that they would not, but I gave none. I wasn't quite sure myself what new twist this had introduced to the relationship. Probably more frightened by what I didn't say than what I possibly would say, she hurried on and continued.

"Because you know me, Kev. You know I'm not like those other people. I love you and I respect you and I want to be with you. You know that, don't you?"

"Yeah, Chris" I lied again, "I know you do."

I rolled off the bed and grabbed my beer that still sat on the windowsill. I killed what was left of it and emitted a satisfying "ahhh."

"What are you drinking?" she asked.

"A beer."

"Sounds good."

"It's very good."

"I was about to have one myself. Take a long, hot shower, get a cold beer, and sit out on the balcony."

"That sounds nice." I said rather indifferently, almost detached.

"Why don't you drive up, Kev. I've missed you while I was gone. All I kept thinking when I was away was how I hate to come home to an empty house. I'm getting really tired of that, you know? I was thinking how nice it would be to come home and have somebody there, have you there, waiting to take me in your arms and give me something real to hold onto."

"That sounds nice."

"So why don't you come up, Kev. We can take a shower and sit outside with a cold beer and just relax. Take our minds off of everything. I got the few days away that I needed and you got your car. No need in dwelling on the past, Kev. Just be glad it worked out in your favor and move on."

"Yeah, move on," I said in the same detached way.

"Go hop in that nice new car and come see me. I'll make you feel better. You know I will. Don't I always make you feel better?"

"I wish I could, Chris. Really, I do. But it's been a very long week. I have hardly eaten or slept. I think I'll just fix dinner and jump in the bed."

"Come up. I'll fix dinner for you and then you can get in my bed. I'm a little tired myself. A nap would do me some good as well."

"I'm sorry," I said, "But I can't. Not today. Maybe we can get together tomorrow."

Chris let out her weary, impatient sigh.

"Okay, Kev. Give me a call tomorow if you want to see me. Give me a call even if you don't."

I hung up the phone and went to the kitchen for another beer. Sitting outside on the patio, my feet thrown up into the other chair Chris had sat in so many times before, I tried not to be angry. But I knew anger was the only emotion strong enough to keep back the hurt, and I wasn't going to be hurt. I couldn't afford to be hurt at that moment. There were still too many things left to be placed into perspective.

How could I have not seen it, I thought. But, oh, I did see it, I told myself. From the very beginning there were bits and pieces here and there, some of which I recognized and heeded, others I treated as Chris would have treated them by looking the other way and pretending whatever I thought I may have heard or seen simply was not so. But the tell-tale signs had been there all along. There was no doubt about that. The only question that remained was what was I going to do about it.

Surely I could not stay with this woman, I tried to reason. How could I possibly stay with a woman who doesn't understand, and doesn't want to understand, what I must face everyday I leave the house in the morning? How could I possibly love a woman so much or love myself so little that I'm willing to deal with the stresses of being young and Black in America and then have to come home and face the same stress under a different guise? How could I possibly lay in the sanctity of my bed each night with a woman I'm not sure I trust any longer or had ever really trusted at all?

It seems that an answer would have come quite easy. But all faults and twisted thinking aside, this was still a woman I loved, and it's not so easy to walk away from love even if it is the best thing to do. And was walking away really the best thing? I wondered. I had tried it once before and it didn't work. I pondered whether turning my back on it all may have been too impulsive, too much of a reaction rather than a decision. *After all, I said to myself, I never expected her to understand, but only to try to understand, to show a little empathy. Surely that's something that must come with time.*

These damn emotions, I thought. They could really get a person in trouble. There I was six months into the relationship when everything started coming out. I sat on the patio relishing the beer as my heart and mind continued their ongoing battle. *What does one do, Kev? What does one do?*

I threw the question to the wind but received no true answer. All that came back to me was the deafening silence, behind which I could faintly hear the quiet—very, very quiet—voice whispering from the pit of my soul, "Wake up, wake up, wherever you are."

Chapter Seventeen

Chris and I were standing in the backyard talking. Standing in the backyard where I had grown up as a child. The weeds were tall, and, as we were very far back, the house was only partially visible. I could not hear the words exchanged but I could see our mouths moving. Mostly Chris's mouth. Snakes. There were snakes in the backyard, and I had gone out to kill them. I could not see where they came from or where they were going. Seemingly out of an invisible hole in time, a brightly colored coral would slither across the ground and then disappear just as quickly as it had come: striped, red, purple, and yellow the snake seemed to taunt me as if some how knowing that it was only an ostensible threat that I posed. Chris never seemed to notice but kept right on talking her mouth moving slow and methodical. I hurled a rock at one of the snakes with determination of ridding the yard of the unwanted trespassers. That was when I saw the large rock standing as a guard and shelter next to the hole into which they descended. They were descending back into that hole. Gasoline, I thought. I would pour gasoline into the dark hole and burn them, hissing sounds came up out of the darkness as if the cold-blooded creatures had somehow read my mind. Louder. The hissing grew louder and I knew they would come. Without thinking, as though encouraged by a primal fear, I ran toward the safety of the house. Ran up out of the darkness. I heard the swishing, slithering sound as it matched me step for step and then gained incredible momentum.

Looking over my shoulder I saw a flash of Chris's ghostly white face staring blankly. The snake was at least fifty feet long and fat. Seemingly unreal. A false creation in a make-believe story. A flash of Chris as if she herself were the queen snake and on me closing in faster and faster. I ran though the door trembling hands fumbling with the lock. Swish and slither. Slammed the door and released the fear but I could hear the queen snake just beyond the door a deafening sound rose up; *crunch crunch crunch*. My cocker spaniel yelped. *Crunch crunch* as the snake ripped at and devoured her fury little body. I stood helpless and frozen the sound of ripping flesh and crunching bone loud in my head.

I awoke with dampness around the collar of my T-shirt. My lip was cut. There was a faint taste of blood in my mouth. I realized I must have bitten it in a fitful state of fear. I laid still in the safety of my bed as reality drifted in and assured me that it was only a nightmare. But I wasn't certain. My bed was slightly vibrating, a low thump was emitted from the wall. Had the nightmare become real? Had the queen snake slithered from my mind and lay in wait beneath my bed? Heavy slumber slowly drifted away and I realized it was only the couple above me. He had probably just beaten his wife and was now screwing her.

That was the routine, as sick as it was. Kick her ass, screw her, kick her ass, screw her. The subtle vibration subsided and the dull thumping noise overhead faded to nothing. I too was fading. Fading back to a place in time where sleep never came easy.

Chapter Eighteen

All I saw was white, and it made me sick and tired. I sat staring at a blank piece of paper and tried to make the words come. But they would not and had not come in quite some time. It occurred to me as I tried to resurrect my dead muse that I had not finished writing anything since I started seeing Chris. The realization terrified me. Having learned the discipline of writing every day, I wondered if I would even be able to find my voice after a six–month hiatus. And, if so, would it take just as long to undo the damage that had obviously been done.

Chris had given me a bound journal for Valentine's Day. It was gray, like her eyes, and the cover was embossed with a golden sun and little stars circling it. The inscription read: "Love—Always and Deeply—Chris." It sat on a closet shelf without a single entry. Certainly there had been little thoughts I had wanted to make note of; there had even been larger issues and ideas I considered developing into full essays. But that was the extent of my creative gesture. I simply considered things from time to time.

What I found interesting about the change that had come over me was that despite it being such a marked contrast to the period prior to meeting Chris, I never even saw it coming. I had been writing every day for several years, having gone through a very prolific stage in which I was easily turning out two or three thousand words a day. I had a one-act play produced at Howard University and a full-length piece given a stage reading. I had enrolled in a writing workshop and was working on my first book. The writing was going well and I had the focus and direction I needed to turn what was once a dream into reality. It wasn't long after I stopped teaching that I was published in *Essence* magazine and then turned right around and landed a piece with *Upscale* magazine. *It was about to happen,* I thought to myself. It was about to happen. That's when the writing came to an abrupt, albeit silent, halt.

I had been working on a collection of essays when Chris and I first got together in January, and had very definitive plans of completing it as my workshop project. Yet I sat there that day with half of the course completed and the book nowhere near finished. I couldn't seem to write anymore and, worse, didn't seem to possess the desire to write anymore. Even my writing instructor had noticed the change in me.

Just write anything, I told myself. Put pen to paper and the rhythm will come back. It's no different than getting on a swing for the first time in fifteen years. All one has to do is jump on and bring the buried instinct back to life. *Come to me, my muse. Come I say, come!*

Nothing. Silence. A white canvas of blank paper. My mind, no matter how hard I tried to fix it on some striking image or a stirring emotion or an interesting snatch of conversation I had overheard, would not let me get past thoughts of Chris.

Memorial Day weekend was right around the corner and we had made plans to attend the annual Jazz Festival in Grant Park. I caught it every year and usually had a really nice time. Chris said that she and a girlfriend had gone one summer and had both found it peculiar that there were no Whites in attendance. I gave her a polite smile and thought, *Yes, can you believe it? We actually gather among our own selves to listen to our own music without a bunch of outsiders invading and trespassing all over our shit. How very, very peculiar indeed.*

All amusement aside, I can't actually say that I was looking forward to the afternoon. The festival had always been nice the previous times I went. Lying on the grass listening to good music and drinking good beer. I was hoping it could be just as nice with Chris lying next to me as the late afternoon sun slowly fell between that thin crack where Earth meets sky. But of course I was thinking about the incident surrounding my car and that strange, strange face she had shown me. My concern was that the feeling that I had settled and compromised so much of what I believed in was so strong that others would feel it as well. I was concerned that everyone who looked at me would know my secret, would know that the woman I flaunted on my arm was an imposter who, by claiming not to see me as a Black man, in so many ways really didn't see me at all. They would snicker and whisper beneath their breaths, the more bold ones probably pointing a derisive finger. No doubt about it, I was going to be exposed.

Regardless, there was still a part of me that felt guilty, almost obligatory, for having dumped Chris on her birthday and refusing to take her to the concert. Wanting to make this up to her, I was willing to risk a few hours of discomfort if doing so was going to make her happy. And it was going to make her happy. She reminded me every day leading up to the festival and pleaded with the rain gods not to show their temperament. The gods obviously weren't listening, as dark clouds moved in late Saturday and rained out the event.

We arrived at the park and found that most people had already dispersed, a few others still lingering around the parking lot or gathering their belongings. I saw and felt the terrible disappointment Chris wore on her shoulders like a heavy shawl. She slumped up against me and threw her arm around my waist.

"Why does this always happen to us?" she asked. "All I wanted was to sit back and listen to some nice jazz. Nothing big. I never ask for anything big, and yet I still come away feeling cheated."

Seeing her like that and hearing the melancholy tone in her voice, I couldn't help but feel a little sorry for her. But such emotions that day in the park, as were most emotions concerning Chris, were very mixed. I felt pity for her and relief for myself. Just like that, with the bursting of a rain cloud, the weight of a million staring eyes had been lifted off of me, the only weight now being that of Chris as she nestled her side into me as though we were Siamese twins.

Chris and I found a low brick wall that had either escaped the rain or simply dried under the scattered rays of sun that peeked from behind drifting clouds. There we sat and talked and drank the beer we brought. It wasn't the day we planned, but it somehow turned out just fine. Once we had laughed enough and played enough, she and I wrapped ourselves around each other and started back for the car. I looked into her face and immediately recognized the familiar look of contentment. Chris had found happiness in spite of the rain. It was the simple things she enjoyed most. The very simple things, like sitting in the park talking and laughing and drinking a beer.

Although I had escaped what was destined to be a rather unpleasant day in the park, I knew that other occasions were bound to arise in which fate would not step in and lend a helping hand. I was either going to have to deal with my feelings, which at this point were bordering on embarrassment, or I would have no choice but to once again try to walk away from the relationship. Whatever choice I made would have to be made soon.

My birthday was only a week away and Chris had already begun to ask me how I wanted to spend it. I tried insinuating that it was no big deal, that turning twenty-four simply marked another year in the life of Kev. But Chris wasn't about to go for that "it's just another day" claim. Birthdays were special to her, her own as well as those close people around her, and she had every intention on sharing it with me.

The first week of June also marked Jackie's birthday. I had thought about sending her a card but was afraid that doing so would remind her of what I had done and only make matters worse. Things between us were already bad, and I was still waiting and hoping that if I laid low for a while that maybe she would eventually forgive me and that we could at least be civil toward one another. But the tension that remained between us was thick. I don't know how many times I passed her around campus and she simply acted as though I weren't even there. I tried to make eye contact, even tried to step into her oncoming path, but Jackie would keep her eyes fixed blankly in front of her and never once flinch.

Such a cold attitude was shared by most of the Black women in the workshop. Everyone pretty much knew the way the story had unfolded. They knew that I spent several months pursuing Jackie until finally able to get next to her and we started dating. They knew that Chris and I had started talking, presumably with more in mind than conversation, and that Jackie wasn't at all too happy about this. They knew that after a few months, Jackie and I split and soon thereafter I started seeing the woman I was accused of having been seeing all along. And the Black women didn't like it. Several of them stopped speaking to me altogether. Like Jackie, they would walk right past me as if I were invisible. Worse, it was as if they did see me but held so much contempt for me that it was beneath them to even look my way.

Conversely, there were a few White women

around campus who had never bothered to say so much as hello but who now seemed to go out of their way to speak. One woman's conversation with me was so uninhibited and suggestive that she may as well had taken off her panties and thrown them at me. It was as if my seeing Chris was affirmation that I was "into White women" and that it was okay if what should have otherwise been a casual exchange of words took on sexual innuendo. And I admit I was offended by it all. I was offended that some of the sisters would write me off so easily because of whom I chose to date and that some of the White women would make such wide, sweeping generalizations about who I was and what I was "into." But unlike so many things with Chris and me that held the potential for disaster, my birthday actually turned out to be another shared moment that I look back on and can't help but smile. We went to Six Flags and spent the afternoon riding upside-down rollercoasters, playing games and taking horrible pictures in one of those photo booths.

I suppose the light mood that day was a further extension of the afternoon we had spent in the park riding the swings. We walked around holding hands and pressed close to each other. It was one of those special times when nothing else mattered, when I felt like I had fallen in love all over again.

Later that evening we went back to her place, drank a beer and then went for a late night swim. The pool at Chris's apartment was empty, as it usually was, and gave me ample room to teach her a few strokes that she'd been wanting to learn. Flinging her arms in an unrefined motion, her body slowly sinking like a descending submarine, Chris would make it to the other side of the pool, wipe the streaming water from her face and exclaim, "I did it, Kev! I did it!"

Her simplicity was so striking that all I could do was return her excitement with a smile, all the time wondering how someone could exist in this rude and callous society for twenty-three years and still possess an innocence so natural and so real.

After our swim we went back to my place, had a few more beers and went to bed. She and I awoke the next morning and started the day with a round of really good sex. Later, as we sat in IHOP waiting for the waitress to return with our breakfast, Chris commented that the sex we had was too good.

"What is too good sex?" I asked.

"It's something rare, something you don't find very often. It's addicting."

I considered this for a moment.

"Addictive," I corrected her.

"You know what I mean,Kev."

Yes, I knew exactly what she meant. I had known this for a very long time, perhaps as far back as Super Bowl Sunday when she admitted that she had been "wanting to do this for a very long time." I didn't know what it was, at least not in an outwardly definitive way, but I could sense that what we had shared that day, and what we shared each subsequent time we got together, was not ordinary sex. Not necessarily the act itself, but the much deeper meaning and symbolic gesture behind it.

"Chris," I recall having said, "I don't know what it is, but lately I've been feeling like I'm not totally myself, like I'm not me anymore."

"What are you talking about?"

"I don't really know how to explain it. It just feels like I'm not whole anymore, like a part of who I used to be has somehow been sucked away from me."

"Kev, you aren't making any sense."

"I know," I said. "I know, but that's how I feel."

"Like you're not yourself?"

"Yeah."

"Like you're not yourself how, Kev?"

"I don't know," I said. "I can't really explain it."

That feeling never went away. Actually, it had intensified over the last couple of months. It had intensified so much that not only could I feel this strange undercurrent in the sex we shared, but Chris had become aware of it as well. Sitting at breakfast with her that morning, I tried to once more attach meaning to what I had been feeling for so long.

"Yeah," I said. "I do know what you mean by our sex being addictive. I think that's what I was trying to tell you earlier."

Chris scrunched up her face. She didn't have to say anything. I had seen the look so many times in the past and knew right away she had no clue of what I was talking about.

"About a month ago I expressed to you my feeling that I wasn't myself, that it seemed as if a part of me was being sucked away."

The muscles around her mouth and eyes relaxed a little. "I vaguely remember you saying something like that. But I don't see what that has to do with sex."

I hesitated before going on as the waitress

returned and began placing our food on the table.

"I think that's what I've been feeling all along, Chris."

"What's that?" she said, dividing her attention between me and her omelet.

"Remember how you once said I make you feel whole, that since we've been together that you've felt like you're able to find yourself and that being with me sort of makes you feel alive?"

"Um-hm. I remember."

"Well, I believe that, Chris. I believe it all."

"You should believe it, Kev. It's true. Before I met you I had retreated back into that hole I was telling you about. I don't know how long I've been there. And then you came along and you gave me a little life, you helped pull me out of that hole. It seems like everyday I come out of that dark hole just a little bit more. Being with you really has helped me find myself."

"I know," I said. "That's what I've been trying to say all along. That the relationship is giving you life but it's doing just the opposite to me. It's actually sucking and draining life from me."

"What are you talking about, draining life from you?"

"I've felt this way for some time, Chris, and I've sort of seen it. I see how happy and energetic and alive you've been since we got together. You are growing and becoming whole. But it's all at my expense, Chris. You're becoming whole because you're literally taking a part of me and feeding off of it. It's like I'm your host, like you've attached onto me and are sort of living through me."

Chris was wearing an incredulous look on her face, the same look she probably donned when I told her about my car shopping experience. Then she said it: "Do you realize what you're saying, Kev? And how ridiculous it all sounds?"

Then she threw at me that strained laughter in hopes that I wouldn't see. But it was too late. I could see the fear in her eyes that I had found her out, that I realized all of the things she did for me weren't for me at all, but were actually for herself. She cooked for me and washed for me and tended to me because she knew that would keep me around, and it was essential for her own growth and development that she kept me nearby. She was a parasite and I was her host. She knew how much turmoil being with her had caused me, but it really didn't matter. Chris was only thinking about her own well-being. She was still laughing in my face.

"Kev," she went on, "I really wish you could hear yourself sometimes. It's like you're suggesting I'm a leech or something and that I've latched onto you and won't let go."

"You find all of this funny, Chris?"

"No, not funny. Just ridiculous. It's all so very ridiculous."

"And I suppose this is in my head as well, that I'm only imagining this?"

"I don't know, Kev. I really don't know."

That was Chris's way of dismissing things when she had enough. She then returned her attention back to her breakfast without another word. Obviously I couldn't turn my head and pretend none of it was so.

Maybe earlier in the relationship I could've deluded myself into thinking I was over analyzing, that I was making too big a deal over something very insignificant. In fact, I had done so more times than I was willing to admit. But not anymore. Too many things had happened so that to ignore them would not have made me a fool in love, but simply a fool.

I knew all too well that what I had been feeling was a sort of erosive process that Chris had introduced into my life. I also knew its connection to the sex we shared. I mentioned to Chris that I felt as if she were sucking the life out of me. Literally speaking, she was doing just that. Each time she got on her knees and went down on me, her oral gesture drew me in just a little closer and made the addiction that much stronger. Certainly there were true emotions and feelings shared between us, but it was, and always had been, the sex that formed the basis of our relationship.

The sex aside, Chris had also begun to take away so much of who I was because she had no real sense of self, purpose or direction in life. I often asked her what she wanted in this world, and her reply was always "I don't know, Kev. I'm not sure what I'm supposed to be doing." Not knowing what she was supposed to be doing or what her "Thing" was in life, Chris subsequently made me her thing. All her attentiveness and caring and outward gestures actually gave her a purpose. Yet making me her "Thing" had robbed me of my own "Thing."

There was no clearer indication of this thievery than my sitting there that day staring at a blank piece of paper. My "Thing" had always been writing. It wasn't an occasional hobby or a way in which I spent idle time. It was who I was and how I defined myself. It was an extension of me, something that I had to do. I had even lost a few girlfriends over my creative pursuits. Not understanding the dynamics that went into writing, the solitary and often reclusive hours that it required, women had given me ultimatums to choose between them and my art. Without hesitation, it was good bye to the women, always firmly embracing the medium through which I found my life force.

But somewhere along the way Chris had stolen my life force from me. I had silently and unknowingly lost a very large part of who I was in the process of getting next to this woman. The closer we got, the harder she sucked, and the more of my soul she took with her. I couldn't help but liken her to a cat. I had heard tales in which cats, when left in a room with a sleeping child, would jump on the child's face and smother it, literally stealing its breath and its life.

Chris, the gray-eyed feline, I thought, slowly stalking around and lying in wait until the moment of opportunity had presented itself. I realized such a moment was now. This was my payback for all of the ways Chris kept me happy and made me feel so good. It was a very large debt I owed, and by no means was she going to let me default on the loan. I felt like a modern-day Faustus. I had sold my soul to the Devil and now he was swooping down on me to make good on the deal.

I sat staring at that blank piece of paper for what must have been a full hour, trying, with whatever part of me was left, to find my muse, find my voice, find myself. But nothing came out of me; there was nothing left of me to give, my soul seemingly as bare and empty as the sheet of white paper. Determined to write something, I picked up my Parker fountain pen and slowly wrote, almost etched, onto the paper: "Shit."

Chapter Nineteen

"Flip that off," she said. "I'm so sick of this."

"Sick of what?"

"All of this," she said while gesturing toward the television. "Every time I flip on the T.V., that's all they're talking about. I don't see what the big deal is anyway. It was just one isolated incident."

"What?" I said.

Chris looked over at me with her mouth slightly ajar. I could see it in her eyes. She had forgotten who she was talking to and inadvertently voiced her feelings about the Rodney King beating. She knew she had stepped over the line she tried every day to stay behind. There was no turning back now, her flippant dismissal bound to throw us into one of those "heavy" discussions she dreaded more than anything else.

"What do you mean isolated?" I asked.

"Come on, Kev. Let's not get into this. All it's going to do is get you upset and lead to an argument."

Chris flipped off the T.V. and walked into the kitchen. She started banging pots and pans on the stove as she began getting everything ready for breakfast. I was still sitting in the living room.

"Chris," I yelled over the kitchen noise, "I asked you a question."

"What, Kev?"

"I want to know why you're so quick to dismiss what happened as isolated."

"Because it was. Stuff like that doesn't happen every day."

"We don't see it every day."

"What is that supposed to mean?"

"It means that what happened to Rodney King is not an exception. That shit isn't new. The only thing new is that somebody happened to catch it on video."

Chris quickly snapped her head in my direction. There was a touch of mockery in her voice.

"Has it ever happened to you, Kev? Have you ever been beaten by the police?" The faint smirk on her face told me that she knew the answer to the question before asking it.

"No," I admitted, "I've never been beaten by the police."

Chris turned her attention back to the non-threatening task of preparing scrambled eggs and French toast. There was a strange sense of satisfaction about her. It was all that simple to Chris. I had never experienced what Rodney King had gone through and so, in her opinion, I had nothing to say about it. But it wasn't necessary for me to have actually been beaten by the police to understand the significance of the King incident. I had certainly had my occasions of being pulled over for nothing more than "probable suspicion." I had once been forced to lie on the ground at gun point while my identification was being verified. I knew what it was like to have a cop trailing me for several blocks daring me to make the slightest infraction.

While the Rodney King incident may have elicited shock from the American people, it was nothing more to me than a visual reminder of just how precarious my existence in this society truly was. Every blow delivered, every kick and punch suggested that Rodney King—that me and every other Black man in this country—was not afforded the same rights as other citizens. It suggested that each day that I left my house I stood the chance of getting my ass kicked for no other reason than perhaps a frustrated cop not having gotten any pussy the night before.

The scary thing about such a reality is that there are no defining parameters. I am no different than Rodney King. Detained on the roadside in the pitch darkness of night, I am not viewed as an individual. An officer does not see my education. He does not see my consistent work history, my clean police record, my sense of values and strong ethics. All he sees is a Black man.

That was all the jury saw as well. The disturbing truth of what had taken place that night, and so many other nights, stared at us from our television screens. Still, this was not enough for a jury to deliver a guilty verdict. They had resorted to what they had become accustomed to their whole lives. They had looked the other way, they had seen only what they wanted to see, they had exercised their racial fears and prejudices by assuming that Rodney King, based on nothing more than his race and gender, must have incited the ass kicking. The defending officers were not on trial. Rodney King was on trial.

It was a 90's version of Emmett Till, a rewriting of Bigger Thomas. It was a modern-day execution. Rodney King never stood a fair chance. From the very moment he was delivered into the world, his fate had already begun to unravel toward that one horrible night. In just a matter of minutes, his inalienable rights as an American citizen would be discredited and nullified. He would be tried, convicted, and sentenced in less time than it takes most of us to collect our garbage and walk it to the curb. He was lucky he had not been killed.

"Tell me something," I said.

Chris continued beating the eggs without acknowledging me.

"Do you think any of this would have happened had he been White?"

Chris slammed the bowl on the counter and faced me. She smoothed her hair from her eyes with her left hand while still holding the beater with her right. A thin stream of egg slowly dribbled onto the linoleum floor.

"See," she said. "I knew you were going to do this. I knew you had to go and attach race to all of this. It can't just be an issue of police brutality. You have to make it into a racial thing. That's all you think about, Kev. Race, race, race. You're consumed by it."

"I'm not consumed by anything. I'm just aware, that's all. I'm aware of everything that's going on around me and I'm not afraid to admit it. I'm not afraid to stand up for my convictions and express what I believe in, which is more than I can say for you and all the many others just like you."

"Whatever, Kev. Whatever."

"You're so quick to point out my problem with being hung-up on race. What about your own problem?"

"What problem is that?"

"Don't play naive, Chris. You know exactly what problem I'm talking about. The problem you and so many other Whites have with embracing reality rather than living in this fantastical illusion that every damn thing is hunky-dory."

"Whatever, Kev."

"But it's not. If anything, race relations in this country are worse now than they were forty or fifty years ago. They're worse because of people like you, people who perpetuate the disease with tight-lipped silence, with averted eyes and deaf ears. People who say one thing but deep down inside believe just the opposite. You pretend you don't see it or hear it and it goes uncontested, it becomes passively condoned. You and everyone like you try to hide behind your little facades and fronts while this malignant disease becomes more and more ingrained upon society and will ultimately dictate the way we perceive and interact with one another."

"I'm not the problem," she said. "You're the problem, Kev. You and Farrakhan and all of these other young Blacks who are so angry and so anti-White. You all are the problem, not me."

My God, I thought, the woman is comparing me to Farrakhan. But she probably hadn't even heard the man speak, her perception of him founded on the politically-biased views expressed in the media. I realized she was not only blind but also deaf. Nothing I said that day, or any day for that matter, had made an impression on her. Chris had closed her mind a very long time ago and had no immediate plans of reopening shop. It was all an exercise in futility. I was wasting my breath, my energy and my time. And I knew that to stay with a woman so out of touch with the real world would be wasting my life. For not only was it evident she wasn't willing to step into my world and try to see things through a broader, more realistic perspective, but each day that I was with Chris I ran the risk of actually being sucked into her little world of make-believe fantasy.

I had seen how easily a very significant part of who I was had already been lost along the way. It wasn't too farfetched that, given time, I would be exposing that same bullshit rhetoric. I could hear myself now talking about, "See, Brother, that's your problem. You spend too much time looking over your shoulder instead of keeping your eyes fixed in front of you. That White man behind you isn't going to throw out his leg and try to trip you up. Stop being so paranoid. You went to a fine institution and got your MBA. So what if there are a few Whites with less experience, less education and less potential applying for the same job. This is '93 not '63. Hadn't you heard? Discrimination is dead. Racism is a thing of the past. Look ahead, my Brother. There's nothing behind you now but skeletons hanging in Jim Crow's closet. America is the land of opportunity. It doesn't want to hear all of that old Black bullshit. Leave that to those stupid niggers who don't want a piece of this American pie, those stupid niggers who would rather sit around flapping their lips and crying about The Man did this and The Man did that. Come, my brother, sit at the table and have a piece of pie."

"Guess you're right," I said. "It seems this is the one subject we can't discuss without it leading to an argument."

"Then we just won't discuss it. We can't discuss it. Not if we plan on being together."

"Is that an ultimatum?"

"Of course not."

"Are you implying that I have to make a choice, Chris? That in order to be with you I must bite my tongue and pretend the world in which I live is not so? Huh? Is that what you're telling me?"

"I'm not telling you anything," she said. "I'm simply pointing out to you that this is a topic we don't agree on and will never agree on. So it's best if it's left untouched."

Listen to what the woman is saying, I told myself. *She doesn't agree with you and will never agree with you. Sure, she'll fuck you and cook for you and walk at your heels like a shadow. She'll even marry you and bear your child. But she absolutely refuses to acknowledge who you are and the life you live. Wake up, Kev. WAKE YOUR ASS UP!*

Realizing it was all a waste of time, I didn't bother to explore the issue any further. I gave Chris exactly what she wanted; I gave her silence. I sat at the table and picked over my breakfast without much more than an occasional "um-hm" as she went on and on about nothing that really mattered one way or the other. I left soon thereafter and drove directly to class.

As if things hadn't been bad enough already, my professor approached me after class and said that he needed to see me in his office. I assumed it was something related to my writing. Perhaps he thought it was time we sat down and discussed my obviously declining classroom performance. What I would learn was that it really wasn't about my writing at all. Professor Bennet told me to close the door behind me and have a seat.

"Kevin," he began, "I really regret that I have to ask you about your personal affairs like this."

Personal affairs? What personal affair did I have that would warrant a closed-door discussion?

"But as I understand it, there's this young lady whom you've been seeing. Chris, I believe it is."

"Yeah," I said, wondering what my relationship with Chris had to do with anything.

"As I said, I really regret having to pry into your business like this. But, well, it seems that your lady friend has expressed an interest in joining the workshop. Do you know anything about that?"

"Yeah, she's mentioned it to me."

"Now of course I can't forbid anyone from enrolling in the program if they so desire. But I still thought I should let you know that someone has expressed to me that she would feel uncomfortable in the same classroom as, um, Chris."

"You're obviously talking about Jackie," I said.

Professor Bennet nodded slowly .

"Well, professor, to be honest I really don't think this is any of Jackie's business."

"It may not be any of her business whom you choose to date, but as instructor of this program, it is part of my job to maintain an atmosphere conducive to writing. And if she's going to be uncomfortable about what's going on with you and this other woman then I need to address that."

"Yeah," I said, "I guess I see your point."

Chris and I had discussed her joining the workshop a while ago and had even considered the possible problems that may have arisen with Jackie. But this wasn't at all what I had in mind. If anything, I thought she may have confronted me or, if she got really bold, confronted Chris. It never occurred to me that she would run to our instructor whining about how uncomfortable Chris's presence was going to make her.

"Jackie's a good writer," Professor Bennet continued. "I would hate to lose her over something like this."

"She's threatened to drop out?"

"Not directly. But she did infer that she didn't think she could continue with the program if Chris were to enroll."

I tried to maintain a very composed outward appearance, although inside I could feel the anger twisting and turning. It wasn't necessarily Jackie's butting her nose in my and Chris's business that bothered me so. I could understand her concern. As just about everyone in the workshop knew of our past together, I'm sure her fear was quite real that Chris and

I would sit around talking and laughing and joking in her face, thus making her look more foolish than she claimed I had already made her look. But in no way would I have been so rude and insensitive. I still cared about Jackie and realized how low-down and tasteless it would have been for me to flaunt my relationship with Chris in her face. I could understand her fear.

What pissed me off, though, was that her going to our instructor with all of this was admission to just how threatened she felt by Chris. As Jackie was extremely shy, I could only imagine how much effort it was for her to find the courage to go into Professor Bennet's office, look this man in the face and show him all of the weakness and insecurity this White woman had brought out of her. Although Jackie was reticent to the point of rarely approaching our instructor, the threat that Chris posed to her was so strong that it had her doing the unthinkable.

It both upset and hurt me that this woman, whom I had always considered to have a stronger will, heart, and disposition than Chris, had been reduced to a pile of quivering jelly. Not only would our instructor know of her weakness, but I was sure that the other students would eventually find out as well. I could not believe that Jackie would openly admit to everyone that this other woman, this other White woman, had such control over her emotions, had somehow touched into her deepest fears, that she was actually contemplating dropping out of the workshop to get away from it all.

Professor Bennet said that it wasn't his decision whether or not to admit Chris to the program but that he would have to pass it on to the department chair. I tried to assure him that there would be no problem, that Chris wasn't trying to join the program to throw everything in Jackie's face but that this was something she was sincerely interested in pursuing.

Although Chris had recently completed her under-graduate studies in speech pathology, she often said that her true heart was not in it as she still entertained the idea of writing the next great American novel. It was in getting to know me, she said, that she realized just how much she did want to write. Professor Bennet apolo-gized once more for having to discuss my personal life.

"But that's what sometimes happens when you find yourself in these triangles," he said. "You get these misunderstandings and complicated situations."

He was right; it had turned into a mess. I left the office and took a seat outside in the yard to get some fresh air and clear my head. Things were bad, I admitted, a sick feeling in my stomach that they would only get worse.

Having always been one to confront my problems, I knew I had no choice but to call Jackie and find out what this was all about. It had been nearly eight months since we'd last spoken and I wasn't sure if she would even accept my phone call. But that was insignificant now. Jackie had traversed the imaginary boundary separating where she and I had stood in the past and where Chris and I now stood in the present. That Chris wanted to enroll in the workshop was none of Jackie's business and it certainly was no business of everyone in class who would relish in seeing how this new twist would play itself out.

Hoping my conversation with Jackie wouldn't be

any more unpleasant than was necessary, I picked up the phone the very next day and punched number seven, which, after all this time, remained encoded on my speed dial.

"Hello?" she said.

It was the first time I had heard her voice since that day she claimed our relationship was nothing but a waste of time and that I had never done anything for her. Although considerable time had passed since then and I had obviously moved on, I had to remind myself why I was calling. It wasn't a social call, I told myself. You aren't calling to see how she's been doing and maybe, by chance, see if the two of you can work things out. Your only reason for calling is to find out why she insists on sticking her nose all up in your business.

"It's Kev," I said. "And I would appreciate it if you didn't hang up."

"I'm not going to hang up."

There was a silence as I pondered her matter-of-fact attitude. Hearing her voice again, minus the bitterness and anger, I suddenly experienced a flash of hope that maybe there was room for reconciliation. I wondered if maybe I had been wrong all along. Maybe she wasn't threatened by Chris at all. Maybe her going to Professor Bennet was her way of telling me that she still cared, that she was still holding onto feelings that she wanted to explore but was simply waiting for me, as always, to "make the first move."

"So what do you want?" she said.

"I want to talk to you."

"Yes, I'm listening."

"I want to talk to you about Chris."

"There's nothing I have to say about that White woman. So if that's the reason..."

"Oh, I think there's a lot you have to say. You certainly shared a great deal with Professor Bennet."

"What are you talking about?" she said.

"You know what I'm talking about. You somehow found out that Chris was interested in joining the workshop and you ran to Professor Bennet crying like a little baby about how uncomfortable it would make you feel being in the same classroom as she."

"So, what's it to you?"

Despite a bit of edginess to my own voice, Jackie still maintained her matter-of-fact demeanor.

"I want to know what right you have going to him discussing me and Chris. That's none of his business, nor is it any of yours."

"It is my business," she said. "I don't want that woman anywhere around me. I don't want to hear her or see her or even be reminded of her."

"Look, Jackie, why don't you get over it, okay? It's been almost eight months now since you and I split. Why don't you find yourself a man and stop worrying about what the fuck I'm doing."

"Nobody's worried about what you're doing. I'm just having my say."

"Oh, so this is what it's all about?" I said. "You have it made up in your mind that Chris is what came between the two of us and so now you're trying to throw some shit our way and mess that up?"

"Mess what up? You don't have anything."

"I have a lot more than I had with you."

"Stop kidding yourself, Kevin. You and I both

know you have nothing."

"I have exactly what I want in my life. Chris is the best thing I've ever had." Jackie gave me a short, derisive laugh.

"I'm the best thing you ever had," she boasted with that knowing assuredness I once found so attractive.

But it wasn't attractive anymore. Jackie had somehow looked straight through me and read all of the secret feelings and emotions I tried to keep locked away. She continued flipping through the pages of my soul like a cheap romance novel.

"I was the woman you wanted then and I'm the woman you want now. It only took a taste of temptation before you realized what you had thrown away."

"Shut up, Jackie. You don't know what you're talking about."

"They say only in darkness can you truly see the light," she plowed right on. "And I'm sure being with that White woman has shown you more darkness than you've ever known in your entire life. Only now are you beginning to see the light. Only now are you beginning to admit to yourself what a fool you've been all of this time."

"You're jealous." I said. "You're jealous and you're threatened."

"Jealous of what?"

"Of Chris. Of our relationship."

She gave me that laugh once more.

"There's nothing to be jealous of, Kevin. Your girlfriend is nothing. Your relationship is nothing. Why are you even sticking up for that White woman? She's nothing."

"She's more woman than you could ever be," I said.

"More woman? Hah! She's a slut. A loose, filthy slut who is just sleeping around every chance she gets. If it weren't you, it would have surely been some other fool. Do you really think you have someone special, someone you can grow with and maybe one day introduce to people as your wife, as Mrs. Luttery? Hah! Don't kid yourself. All you have is just another common, loose, White woman. That was all she was when you first met her and that's all she'll ever be. She's probably off somewhere right now sucking some other man's dick."

"That may be," I said. "But I would much rather have a loose White woman than to waste my time with you...you stinking, Black bitch."

If I had ever been embarrassed about my relationship with Chris, at no time had the embarrassment been as great as it was at that particular moment. Jackie was one of the sweetest, most gentle women I had ever known. "Bitch" was the last word that came to mind whenever I thought of her. And yet I had dared to label her with such an offensive term. Not only had I called her a "bitch," but I called her a "Black bitch." I ascribed color to it. Yet it was obvious she was Black. My pointing this out, particularly under such circumstances, shared a likeness to what a White man would say to suggest her inferiority.

I knew that the words coming out of my mouth weren't my own, the realization of which deeply disturbed me. For I realized that not only was Chris a stranger to me but that in some way I had become a stranger to myself. Something in me had changed. There was a foreign body inside of me that had made itself right at home. It wasn't loud or conspicuous. Instead, it softly stalked around on padded feet, laid low until, no longer able to conceal itself, it leapt forward like a cat in waiting.

"I'm sorry," was all I could say.

I expected Jackie to go off, to just get ridiculous on my ass, but she didn't. She did just the opposite and took a very unexpected stance.

"I'm sorry, too," she said. "I'm sorry this has all happened to you."

I wanted to continue wearing the mask and claim that nothing had happened to me. But it was too late for that. Jackie had already peered behind my outward facade and seen the ugly, twisted face I had assumed since being with Chris. All I could do now was hope that she could somehow forgive me for what seemed unforgivable.

"I wish I could get upset with you," she said, "but I can't. I can't get upset because I realize you aren't altogether yourself. All I can do is suggest you go to church sometime, Kevin. Invite the Lord into your life and ask Him to give you the strength you need to work out whatever is tearing you apart like this."

No, I was thinking, *not this. Anything but this. Curse me out, yell at the top of your lungs, hang up the phone. You can even drive over here and slap me. But please, Jackie, please don't start talking about saving my soul.*

"That's what I did," she went on. "When you and I broke up, I went to the Lord and asked Him to show me the way. And He did. He told me that everything was going to be okay and that you simply aren't the man for me, Kevin. And you aren't. I realize that now. I realize that you are no good for me, that you aren't my soulmate."

"Come on, Jackie. You make it sound like I'm the Devil or something."

"The Devil wears many faces, Kevin. You remember that."

"Sure," I said.

"Because I'm concerned about you," she added. "Believe it or not, despite everything you did to me and even despite what you just called me, I still care about you. And I'm concerned about the way you're living your life. I don't like it, Kevin. I don't like it at all. I keep getting the feeling that something very horrible is going to happen to you if you don't change your lifestyle."

Although I initially thought Jackie's religious speech was simply another attempt at trying to come between me and Chris, I admit her words were pretty frightening. It wasn't so much the words themselves that sort of spooked me, but the mere fact that I could clearly hear the conviction in her voice. She actually believed what she was saying and was speaking directly from the heart. Had I been a more religious man, I probably would have accepted her as a prophet.

"Change what lifestyle?" I asked.

"I think you can answer that for yourself. You know better than I do what's eating away at you like this. All I ask is that you do something about it before it's too late."

"Can I call you sometime?"

"No," she said. "It's best if you don't."

"I just want to talk, Jackie. That's all. I need to talk to you."

"I realize it's been a long time since everything happened between us, but time doesn't change everything. You hurt me all over again. Sure, I got over your cheating on me, and I'll even forgive you. But a little piece of hurt will always be there. I loved you, Kevin. I loved you more than any man I've ever known. But things are different now; we're different now. So it's best if you don't call because there really isn't anything left to say. Just remember everything I said, Kevin, and take good care of yourself."

"Jackie..."

"Good bye," she said and hung up the phone.

There was something in Jackie's "goodbye" that suggested a finality to everything we ever shared. It hurt because I knew Jackie spoke with sincerity when she said I was not the man for her. It hurt even more because I knew everything she said about me and my relationship with Chris was true. I had been kidding myself all along.

I went into my "think spot" and slumped down on the floor. Was it possible that I really was headed toward disaster? I posed the question to myself despite already knowing the answer. *Yeah,* I thought, *things were definitely headed in that direction.* I had seen it present itself in more subtle ways in the past, the recent incident with Jackie only confirmation to the inevitable. Staying in this relationship with Chris was both mentally and emotionally unhealthy. It was understood that I had to separate myself from it all. I only wondered where I would find the strength to walk away from this woman who had crawled inside and begun to consume me.

"Invite the Lord into your life and ask Him to give you the strength," Jackie had said. *Maybe I'll do that,* I told myself. *Maybe I'll do just that.*

It was a little after 6:00 when I finally finished my talk with myself. I had promised Chris I would be at her place by 4:00 so that we could spend a little time lying out by the pool before we went to dinner. I didn't bother to call with an apology for running so late but just jumped in my car and drove up instead. By the time I got there, Chris was wearing a mixed look of suspicion and hurt.

"I didn't think you were coming," she said. "I was beginning to wonder..." Her words drifted off as she turned her back and walked into the bedroom. I stepped inside and followed.

"Wonder what?" I said, slowly, almost cautiously stepping into the bedroom.

For some reason her bed looked larger than usual. It loomed in front of my eyes and commanded full attention. Once very warm and inviting, Chris's bed now looked cold and alien. It looked almost sinister. I felt as if I stood on foreign territory, though I realized Chris and I spent more time in that one room than any other part of her apartment.

"What were you wondering?" I repeated.

Chris walked over and put her arms around my waist. She pressed her body tightly against me and laid her head on my chest.

"I was beginning to wonder if you had left me for another woman."

"No," I said. "Not another woman."

She lifted her face and fixed those eyes on me.

"Kev?"

I didn't say anything.

"Kev, what does that mean, 'not another woman'?"

I peeled her arms from around my waist and took a step backwards, her small wrists clasped between my hands.

"I'm saying I can't be with you anymore, Chris."

She gave me a light smile and flung her hair off her face.

"You don't mean that," she said. "You didn't mean it the last time and I know you don't mean it this time."

"No, Chris, I do mean it. I think we've both known for some time now that it was coming to this."

"Kev, you can't leave me. You need me. Don't you, Kev? Don't you need me in your life?"

"Please, Chris. You aren't making this any easier."

"I need you," she said. "I need you here with me, Kev."

She took a step in my direction and tried to wrap her arms around me. I kept her wrists locked in my hands and maintained distance between us.

"That's the problem," I said. "You need me. And that's a bad sign, Chris. It's a bad sign when you start needing another person to make you feel whole."

Chris pulled away from me and sat on the bed. Her demeanor suddenly changed as I could almost feel the rush of thoughts and emotions flowing through her.

"It's Jackie, isn't it?" she asked, a touch of bitterness

in her voice.

I didn't say anything.

"You're getting back with her, aren't you?"

I slowly shook my head "no" as her gray eyes filled with tears and became even more obscured. Her cheeks were becoming flushed with blood, her bottom lip unable to fight off a slight quiver. I had never truly known what dark hole Chris often talked about being in before getting involved with me. I could only imagine that it was a state of depression or emotional detachment. But seeing her sitting on the bed and seemingly changing right in front of me, it seemed as if I were witnessing her retreat back into that place from which she claimed I had pulled her.

She walked over to me and wrapped her arms tightly around my waist. I didn't object this time but instead returned the embrace and slowly ran a comforting hand up and down her back. Her face was hot and moist as she pressed closer into me, her salty tears freely streaming down her cheeks and fucking up my silk shirt."Don't leave me," she said, her words half choked with tears and half muffled against my chest. "I need you,Kev. I can't do this without you. I can't go back into the hole. I can't go back there, Kev. I just can't."

I remember a time not too long ago when I could have easily pushed Chris away, spat a few harsh words at her and walked out without giving it a second thought. In fact, before Jackie came along that had been the crude and callous manner in which I ended most of my relationships. Like I said, when I was done with a woman I was done with her. I was never one to wallow in a pool of indecision. Once I made up my mind that everything had become a waste of time, there was nothing that could convince me otherwise. Not tears, not promises, not sex. Not even money could stop me in my tracks once I had started for the door.

And I regret that. Not the ability to remove myself from what I recognized to be a state of stagnation. For that's something I hope I always possess. But it's the indifferent and often cruel way in which I dismissed so many women that I now regret. I told myself when I first started seeing Jackie that I wasn't going to do that, that I couldn't continue going through life indifferently flicking people off like a disgusting booger. I knew I could not be with Chris, and I was resolved to walk away from her once and for all. It was a matter of life and death. She was living through the relationship while I was dying. Still, I didn't want to hurt her the way I had hurt so many others in the past. Moreover, I couldn't simply quit this woman cold turkey. It would've been too much of a shock to my system. I knew quite well that Chris wasn't mixing words when she said the sex we shared was addictive. The whole relationship was addictive. Chris needed me, and I was now finally able to admit to myself that I too shared a similar dependency. She was my fix, emotionally and physically, and I had become hooked on her.

I wasn't going to lie to myself and pretend it was going to be easy to kick the habit. I knew that it wasn't. For like any other addiction, Chris was deep in my system and would remain there for some time. There would be moments of craving, withdrawal symptoms and possibly even states of relapse. But I knew I would eventually get her out of my system and that I would regain myself in the process. It wasn't going to happen the next day, the next week, maybe not even the next month. Yet resolution had set in and I had taken the first step on the road to recovery. That day was one of the very few times Chris and I got together and did not engage in sexual activity. I was weaning myself from the addiction.

Chapter Twenty

It had been two weeks since Chris and I last got together. Two long, hard weeks. We still maintained a phone relationship but even that had changed. Conversation had become casual and detached. There was no longer that suggestive innuendo exchanged between us, no longer those tender words that are often the hallmark of two people in love.

We obviously had not formally split, as we still spoke nearly every day, but I didn't feel that we were actually together. Feelings and emotions aside, I knew that I was gradually letting go and that given time the phone calls would dwindle to every other day, a few times a week and then stop altogether. Right now I was simply handling my recovery one day at a time. Then relapse set in.

Withdrawal from Chris was worse than kicking a cocaine habit. It seemed like every song on the radio had a special meaning attached to it. Every conversation I held contained a phrase or joke or observation that I knew she and I would have relished together. My apartment was unbearably quiet, my bed empty. I tossed and turned under the sheets, reaching in vain for what before had always been there to help calm my restless sleep. Strands of her hair littered my bathroom. Her robe still hung in my closet. Her box of tea occupied a space in my kitchen cabinet. And yes, through it all, I was wearing a perpetual hard-on.

We were talking on the phone one day when she offered to come over and fix a pot of curried goat. It was the beginning of the week, perhaps a Tuesday, and we both had the upcoming weekend off from work. Not only did she want to come over and cook dinner, but she suggested she pack a bag and actually spend a couple of days at my place. Although a bit apprehensive, temptation was too much. I thought that I had done well up until that point and that the weaning process allowed for a little taste every now and then until I no longer possessed the desire. So I consented with reservation.

I suppose I should have known that our weekend plans would fail to materialize. That was the fate Chris and I shared. Plans were often ruined unexpectedly. As the Republican party had recently taken over Congress, I had already begun to witness their merciless cutting of affirmative action programs that were deemed unconstitutionally discriminatory. Just that week, the University of California board of regents passed anti-affirmative action measures for admission to its nine campuses. Chris and I were talking on the phone the Saturday she was supposed to come over and spend the weekend. I really didn't think too much about the question as I solicited her opinion about the recent political maneuver.

"I hadn't heard anything about it," she confessed.

I wasn't surprised.

"Yeah," I said, "UCLA just abolished its program this week."

"Kev, what time should I come over?"

"I don't know. About five, I guess."

"Then I should be going," she said.

"Listen, before you go."

"Yeah?"

"I was wondering how you felt about that," I said.

"About what?"

"Affirmative action."

She didn't say anything. Still no surprise on my end. And then:

"Well, Kev, I really don't think about it. So I guess I have no opinion one way or the other."

"But you know what it is, Chris. You know enough to at least have an opinion."

"Do we have to talk about this?" she asked.

"It's just a question," I replied. "No big deal. I'm just curious what you think about it."

"Well, I don't agree with it."

"Why not?"

"Because it's not fair. It's..."

"Reverse discrimination?"

Chris must have heard the sarcasm in my voice as she hesititated for a moment before continuing. I didn't want her to think that I was poking fun at her views and opinions, but I couldn't help noticing how very predictable she had become.

"Yes," she said with a touch of annoyance. "It's reverse discrimination. It's preferential treatment based on race. It's no different than hiring a White person just because they're white."

"I agree."

"You do?" she asked in that incredulous tone of hers.

"Absolutely. It's very unfair that a group of people should benefit from something as arbitrary as skin color."

Chris emitted a light laugh, almost an expression of relief. Then she said, "I never thought you, of all people, would be against affirmative action."

"Oh, I'm not. What I said was that I agree it's unfair to give special treatment to a particular group because of race."

"But, Kev, that's what affirmative action is."

"Yes, I said, and it's unfair. But it's no more unfair then the discrimination so many people would face if it weren't for such programs."

"And does that make it right? Does punishing those of us who aren't racists, who aren't trying to keep Blacks down make it right?"

Just when I thought everything Chris now said and felt was the expected, she changed her face and showed me another side. I could actually detect a hint of emotion in her voice. She wasn't merely speaking from rote memorization, not merely throwing around generic opinions White America keeps conveniently tucked in its back pocket for just such an occasion. She was taking a definitive stance for something she truly believed and felt. The only problem was that her stance was on the wrong side of the tracks.

"Don't ask me if it's right," I said. "I'm in no position to say if it's right or not. But ask me if it's fair and I'll admit that, no it's not fair."

"Then how, Kev? How can you support something that you admit is unfair? It's hypocrisy."

She was growing more impassioned by the second, her conviction to speak out against the injustice affirmative action supposedly imposed upon her people reminding me so much of my own heartfelt emotions. I thought that Chris would have heard the passion accompanying each word she spoke and understood how I too could speak so strongly about that in which I believed. I was silently hoping that maybe she could finally view things through a different perspective, view them through my perspective.

But that was the inherent problem; she could only view the world through her own eyes. And just as I was unable to understand how she could so easily dismiss as fiction so much of what I lived and thus knew to be fact, so, too, was Chris now looking with the same type of vision. She only saw what she had been shown. Through it all, as I listened to her that day, the reality became quite clear that no matter how insistent she was that she despised White culture, that she wasn't "like most White people," Chris did what we are all inclined to do: She sided with her own.

I continued, "I believe in affirmative action because the alternative doesn't work. Sure, if this country weren't so fucked up then there would be no need for such a thing. It would be great if every man was judged on merit alone. But it's not like that. It's never been like that. And the person who thinks it will ever be like that is an idealistic fool."

"So is that your solution to making things equal? When too much prejudice and racism and hatred is placed on one side of the scale, you balance it by placing the same thing on the other side?"

"Do you know any other way?" I asked.

"Well, for starters, people like you can stop being so negative and pessimistic. Things will never get better if you keep saying they won't. I know I can't change the world, Kev. Neither can you. But I'm at least doing my part to make things better."

"What are you talking about?" I said. "Doing your part? The only thing I see you doing is perpetuating the illusion that if we pretend that it's not there then the problem will somehow disappear on its own."

"Believe it or not," she said, "I'm actually making an effort to see some of the things I hear you talking about. I'm trying to do my part by looking at society through a different light."

"Is that so?"

"Yeah, Kev. Just the other day I went out and bought *Mister Man*."

No, I was thinking. *No she didn't.* I know she must have said Superman or Batman or some other fictitious cartoon character. But I know she didn't say she bought *Mister Man*.

"You bought what?" I asked.

"Mister Man. The book. You know it?"

"Of course I know it. But why would you be interested in a book like that?"

"Well," she started, "Like I said, I've been thinking about some of the things you've said to me in the past, some of your feelings and views on things. And I realize that was the main reason you had such a hard time with the relationship. You didn't think I was willing to understand just where you were coming from. But I'm trying to understand now, Kev. I really am."

It was unreal. Were it not for my own hand putting these words onto paper, I never would've believed it. Chris, with her typical White-American mentality, had gone out and purchased an anthology of literary pieces written by a very wide range of Black men. She had reduced me to a sociological study. Like so many others just like her, Chris's response to my world was all so very simple and convenient. The totality of my existence was seemingly so shallow that she could just run out and buy a book or take a class or attend a seminar and, just like that, understand who I was and what I was about. She was playing that social work bullshit and I didn't like it.

"So what is reading that book suppose to do?" I asked.

"It's going to give me a better understanding of how Black men think and feel."

"What do you need to read a book for? I've been telling you for the last seven months how I think and feel. Not a bunch of type on a page, Chris, but real thoughts and emotions. Breathing, living feelings from a real Black man. You've heard me express my thoughts and emotions. You've seen them. You've been in the same room with me and actually felt them. And none of that means anything to you? None of that is real enough for you? Isn't my living twenty-four years in this skin and in this world more authentic than anything you could ever read? Huh, Chris? None of that matters? You need a fucking book to tell you who I am and what I'm about?"

I suppose both of our emotions were running pretty high by that point. Chris was offended that I would champion a program that theoretically was no different or better than the exact thing I despised. And I was offended that she would belittle me, would belittle Blacks in general, by taking such a presumptive stance as to think that the essence of who we are as a people is so simple as to be understood by reading a book.

"I think its best if you don't come by," I said.

"What's wrong, Kev? You lost your appetite again?"

"I've lost a lot more than that," I said. "A lot more."

"What are you complaining about? I'm doing this for you."

"That's what I'm complaining about. You're only feigning interest in all of this to appease me, to make me happy. But you don't give a damn how I feel or what I think. You ran out and bought a book hoping I would take the gesture as a sign of your sincere desire to understand, and that maybe I would give the relationship another chance. But you don't want to understand, Chris. You don't want to be bothered with it at all. This isn't anything you're doing for me, nor is it anything you're doing for yourself out of genuine concern or interest. This is all just another one of your fronts."

"Bravo, Kev. Bravo. You win the prize for the day."

The condescension in her voice was as mocking as

a circus clown. I hung up the phone with a feeling of pure disgust. I didn't want Chris coming over and climbing in my bed. I didn't want to see her face or hear her voice. I didn't want Chris anywhere around me. All of a sudden I understood what Jackie must have felt when she expressed the same sentiment the last time we spoke. Chris was a distraction, and I didn't need any of that in my life.

For the first time since Chris and I had gotten together I was beginning to feel more like myself. My focus and direction were coming back to me. I once again had a definite purpose for getting up each morning. Instead of having Chris over to my place that night, I sat down with pen and paper and started trying to make sense of everything that had transpired over the last year.

As if my muse had never left me, I found myself writing with the same zeal and fervor I once had before Chris drained all of that out of me. It was coming easily and freely. My experience with Jackie and Chris was to be the first essay I'd written in a very long time. Yet the more I wrote, the more in touch I became with so many feelings I never even knew were there. It was then that I realized I could never fully capture the experience in a few thousand words. That night I sat down to write an essay and ended up with a book.

Chapter Twenty-One

would be lying if I said that my last heated conversation with Chris was enough to mark the relationship with a final period. It was not. Time would have to provide the ultimate punctuation. As days blended into weeks and summer slowly faded, so, too, did the relationship fade. Though we hardly ever talked anymore, and never went out, every now and then Chris and I would get together and relieve our sexual tension. Everything having come full circle, the end of the relationship was an exact parallel to the beginning. We were mere sex partners. As painful as such an admission is, in so many ways that's all we ever truly were. Everything else, the deep emotions, strong feelings and mutual sharing, was all parenthetical, all nonessential elements of the relationship set off by orgasm on each end.

In time there would be nothing left between us— no more conversation, no more get-togethers, no more sex. All that remained were memories, momentos and pain. There was a lot of pain. So intense was the pain that I had to fight with myself to keep from dialing her number. But I understood what the consequences doing so posed and was, therefore, better able to exercise self-restraint.

I eventually got over Chris, collected the disjointed pieces of my emotions and moved on with my life. I was once again writing every day. I was writing, in fact, the very book that you now hold in your hands. Of course I could not escape the irony that went along with doing so. My writing about the experience was both a catharsis and a disease. Placing pen to paper helped me to understand what I had gone through, but at the same time it forced me to relive some of the darkest pieces of my past.

By doing so, I willingly embarked upon a journey too many of us would rather not take. It was a journey of self-analysis. I looked into the deepest and darkest recesses of who I am and made an open admission. It is something that we must all do at some point in our lives. For how can we possibly begin to understand one another when, lest we see something we don't like, we refuse to understand ourselves.

Perhaps that is what my relationship with Chris revealed more than anything else. It revealed the deeply-rooted social mores of our society, the attitudes and beliefs we share that paradoxically divide just as readily as they bind.